FINANCING

STATE

GOVERNMENT

IN THE 1990s

Edited by Ronald Snell
National Conference of State Legislatures

NATIONAL CONFERENCE OF STATE LEGISLATURES

NATIONAL GOVERNORS' ASSOCIATION

DECEMBER 1993

National Conference of State Legislatures
William T. Pound, Executive Director
1560 Broadway, Suite 700
Denver, Colorado 80202

444 North Capitol Street, N.W., Suite 515
Washington, D.C. 20001

National Governors' Association
Raymond C. Sheppach, Executive Director
444 North Capitol Street, N.W., Suite 250
Washington, D.C. 20001

The text of this report is printed on recycled paper

CONTENTS

LIST OF TABLES AND FIGURES

PREFACE

This document is a report on current issues in state taxes, a collaborative effort of the staff of five organizations representing state officials: The National Governors' Association (NGA), the National Conference of State Legislatures (NCSL), the Federation of Tax Administrators (FTA), the Multistate Tax Commission (MTC), and the National Association of State Budget Officers (NASBO).

This executive summary and the full report are intended as a summary of conditions affecting state tax systems, an overview of the tax systems themselves, an examination of current problems with an analysis of the causes of those problems, and a range of options that state policymakers might pursue to match state tax systems better with current national economic structures. In keeping with the policy of the report's principal sponsors, NCSL and NGA, the report does not make policy recommendations on specific issues. It raises questions, explains why they are important, and offers a range of possible ways to deal with problems.

The report is directed primarily at state policymakers and their staffs, who will have to address the unavoidable issues the report discusses. Members of public interest groups, local and federal officials, the business community, and taxpayers in general may also find it useful.

The primary editor of the report is Ronald Snell of NCSL, who has also drafted the sections of the main report on trends in government revenue and changes in the economy and demographics. The other major authors of the report are Harley T. Duncan and Ronald Alt of FTA, Dan Bucks and Michael Mazerov of MTC, Harold Hovey of *State Policy Reports*, and Scott Mackey of NCSL. Other significant participants from these organizations have been Tim Masanz of NGA, Martha Fabricius, formerly of NGA, Brian Roherty and Melanie Nowacki of NASBO, and Christopher Zimmerman of NCSL.

The executive directors of the five organizations—Raymond C. Sheppach of NGA, William T. Pound of NCSL, Harley Duncan of FTA, Dan Bucks of MTC, and Brian Roherty of NASBO—have met periodically to discuss drafts with staff. Numerous state officials, university faculty, and legislators advised the five groups at the outset of this undertaking. Public hearings on a draft released in November 1992 elicited a wide range of useful comments from various businesses and public interest groups, for which the sponsors of the report express their gratitude, as they do to all of the participants in this important undertaking.

EXECUTIVE SUMMARY

SECTION 1
THE APPROACHING CRISIS

This report examines the ways that changes in the American economy, the population, and federal policy have undermined the traditional bases of state tax systems and have made state taxes less responsive to economic growth than they were formerly. The changes this report describes have moved state taxes away from equitable treatment of taxpayers, help account for the fiscal difficulties states have encountered in recent years, and will make state finances increasingly difficult to manage unless the underlying changes are addressed. The report suggests possible ways for state governments to address these problems.

The basic design of the tax systems with which states have entered the 1990s dates to the 1930s. They were designed for an economy of smokestack industries that no longer exists. Manufacturing is in decline relative to other areas of the economy. The major growth areas of the economy spring from technologies, processes, and services that did not exist 60 years ago or even 20 years ago. The American population is older and more mobile than before. The federal government is more and more involved in state tax policy. Business activities are increasingly multistate or international in scope. Despite all the revisions of state tax policy in recent years, state governments have not succeeded in modernizing their tax systems to reflect these sweeping changes.

All three of the most important state taxes—the general sales tax, the personal income tax, and the corporate income tax—have to some extent been made obsolete by economic and demographic change. The sales tax and the corporate income tax have been the hardest hit and receive the most attention in this report.

The report uses generally acknowledged principles of good state tax policy as a standard of evaluation. These principles hold that a state tax system should provide appropriate and timely revenues, distribute burdens equitably, promote economic efficiency and growth, be easily administered, and ensure accountability. Although no single tax can comply with all of these criteria, it is important to move toward these principles even though they cannot all be expressed equally.

SECTION 2
PROBLEMS WITH STATE REVENUE SYSTEMS

Interstate tax competition. Interstate tax competition for economic development can undermine state tax bases, produce tax inequities, and inhibit tax reforms without always providing compensatory benefits. All states use tax policy for economic development, and some economists argue that such tax competition is in the best interest of the national economy by encouraging the delivery of services at low costs in order to keep tax rates low. The relationship between tax concessions and economic development is complicated and uncertain, but it is clear that poorly targeted concessions can produce inequitable shifts of the tax burden to less-favored industries or businesses. Interstate competition can have a chilling effect on efforts to reform state tax codes, because of fears of making a state uncompetitive with its neighbors.

Problems with sales and corporate income taxes. As the American economy has shifted from the production and consumption of goods to the production and consumption of services, state sales and corporate income taxes have not kept pace. Sales tax bases have not kept pace: Few states have extended sales taxes to services in any extensive way. Some goods, like groceries, have been excluded from the tax base. There is no simple way to address this issue. Proposals to extend sales taxes to services must solve the difficult issues of tax pyramiding, collection of taxes on interstate transactions, and definitions of services.

The shift also has affected the corporate income tax. Many services are delivered by businesses that are not organized as corporations and so are not subject to the corporate income tax. While the income of partnerships and sole proprietors is subject to personal income tax, the production of services in the nonprofit sector is not subject to taxation at all. While these results may be desirable, they often have occurred without the awareness of policymakers, and without review of the implications for state tax policy.

Another major issue is that the rules most states follow for the apportionment of multistate corporations' income among states for tax purposes are not as readily applicable to corporations that produce or sell services as they are to more traditional goods-producing corporations. One of the consequences is that the goods-producing sector may be forced to bear a disproportionate share of the tax burden. Outdated tax systems can exacerbate the decline of manufacturing industries.

The national and international scope of business activity. Because
state tax systems have not been adapted to the increasingly interstate
and international character of economic activity, state tax systems create
unintended loopholes and provide competitive advantages to some
large interstate and multinational corporations.

Outdated federal policies are also to blame—the *Bellas Hess* rule
limiting a state's power to require an out-of-state firm to collect sales
taxes for the state is one example. But tax structures under a state's
control can present comparable problems, and create legal advantages
for some taxpayers. Some state tax provisions, for example, allow
multistate corporations to shift income from one state to another to avoid
corporate income taxes, which can shift tax burdens inequitably to
businesses that are unable to take advantage of such provisions.

Federal pre-emption of state taxing authority. State tax bases are
being eroded by federal restrictions that are more stringent than the
constitution requires. Federal statutes and judicial decisions have, for
example, pre-empted state power to tax various kinds of real and
personal property in addition to limiting state authority to require
vendors to collect state sales taxes, as already mentioned.

More recently, federal regulatory action has threatened to become a
third path toward pre-empting state tax bases. The possibility of a
federal value added tax or federal intervention in disagreements
between states over their ability to tax commuters could lead to further
erosion of state control of traditional tax bases.

Shift away from property taxes. The shift away from state and local
governments' reliance upon property taxes adds a structural problem of
a different sort to state tax systems. Reduced reliance on property taxes
has made state tax systems less regressive and has reduced fiscal
disparities among local governments, by substituting state sales and
income tax collections for property tax collections. The substitution adds
to the strain on state tax bases, however, making it all the more
important to resolve structural problems with broad-based state taxes.

The personal income tax The personal income tax is in many ways
the most sound of broad-based state taxes, but it, too, suffers from base
erosion. An increasing proportion of American workers' income is paid
in benefits that are not subject to taxation. Various tax preferences,
credits, and exemptions in addition to those the federal government
allows reduce tax base responsiveness to economic growth. Preferential
treatment for elderly people's income without a means test will be more
and more expensive as those over 65 make up a larger share of the
national population. The increasing mobility of Americans creates
compliance problems.

SECTION 3
OPTIONS FOR CHANGE

Interstate tax competition. States are more likely to adopt new tax incentives than they are to repeal what they have. There are, however, ways to ameliorate the undesirable effects of interstate tax competition. It can be done through accurate evaluations of a state's tax climate in comparison with other states, targeting incentives, reviewing the impact of incentives to see whether they reach their goals, and, in the long run, moving toward cooperative policymaking and consistent tax policies.

Sales and use taxes. Although the most common prescription for the ailments of the sales tax is to extend its base to include service transactions, there are some serious side effects. If sales taxes are imposed on services purchased by businesses as part of the production process, pyramiding will occur—taxes will be applied repeatedly in the process of production and be passed to the eventual consumer. Ways exist to resolve this problem with goods; doing so for service transactions is more difficult. Interstate transactions and competitiveness present additional problems more difficult to address in the case of services than of goods. These problems call for caution, but do not prohibit extending the sales tax base to services. The taxation of many consumer services, for example, would present few problems, and there are few technical problems with extending the tax bases to include goods that are now exempt.

Individual income taxes. State individual income taxes are not threatened with obsolescence like corporation income and sales taxes, but they could benefit from updating. States that have not done so should consider coupling their income taxes to the federal base for consistency in treatment of income and simplicity of compliance and administration, even though conformity limits state options. States should review the exclusions and deductions they have added to federal provisions to see whether they have the intended effect, and especially should reconsider preferential treatment of the income of the elderly.

Because personal income taxes are the most progressive feature of state tax systems, serving to offset the regressivity of property and sales taxes, states should evaluate any income tax revisions in light of their effect on the entire tax system.

The need for greater state cooperation in taxation of business. In order to preserve a fair and workable system of business taxes, states need to cooperate in creating and administering business tax policy. Cooperation could prevent duplication of efforts and produce more efficient tax systems, possibly mitigate the effects of state competition for economic development, and help forestall federal pre-emption through more state uniformity.

Value added taxes. At least in theory, state value added taxes (VAT) could cure some of the ills of current state tax systems. A VAT could replace a number of state business taxes (including industry-specific taxes) with one tax, could allow for low tax rates through the use of a broad base, and could resolve a number of problems related to apportionment, application, and equity of existing taxes. There are numerous reasons that it is unlikely states will turn to value added taxes as a replacement for existing taxes.

Problems include the constitutionality of certain forms of a VAT; the possibility—not entirely certain—that a VAT would be regressive; the argument that a VAT is hidden taxation unlike other major forms of taxes; and the fact that a VAT would be payable by businesses operating at a loss since it is not based on profits. Unfamiliarity with the VAT may cause policymakers to exaggerate drawbacks rather than advantages, and value added taxation is likely to attract more attention in the future.

Property taxes. There are a number of ways to improve property tax administration and to address inequities. Market value assessment of property, more training for assessors, and frequent assessment can improve administrative practices. Targeted tax relief and full disclosure practices address some taxpayer issues. States have experimented with a number of means to address disparities in wealth among jurisdictions, including regional tax base sharing and statewide property taxes to equalize education funding.

Preventing federal pre-emption. Cooperative state action is the best way for states to ward off federal pre-emption. Some issues can be addressed by interstate compacts, not all of which require congressional approval. Uniform laws are another potential tool, as states have demonstrated in the widespread enactment of the Uniform Division of Income for Tax Purposes Act (relating to corporations' income). Some issues may require partnership with the federal government. For states to preserve their traditional role in the federal system, they will need to cooperate more extensively and fully than in the past to prevent federal encroachment on tax bases.

INTRODUCTION

I t's time to take a hard look at state tax systems. The public has
increasing doubts about the fairness of taxes as well as the size of
government budgets. There are also questions about whether
elements of state and local tax policies help or hinder economic
development. And, despite the tax increases of recent years, state and
local revenue systems are failing to provide stable and predictable
revenues. This failure was dramatized by the 1990-1991 recession, but it
is becoming clearer that there are long-run structural problems as well.
State systems are becoming obsolete, inequitable, and unresponsive to
changes in the economy. Designed primarily during the 1930s for a
nation of smokestack industries in deep economic depression, state tax
systems fall short in the 1990s when services are supplanting
manufacturing as the economic linchpin, the economy is increasingly
global, and new information-based industries appear almost daily. To
assist state policy makers in understanding these changes and
considering potential solutions, this report examines:

• The current inefficiencies in the structure of state taxes.

• The ways that economic and demographic changes will further
erode the productivity of state tax systems in coming years.

• How federal policies have weakened state tax systems.

• Potential policy solutions.

Nor will economic recovery address taxpayers' weariness or the
continued demand for increases in state spending on health, education,
and law enforcement, which annually absorb larger shares of state tax
revenues. Streamlining service delivery, improved performance
evaluation, and budgeting for results all hold promises of greater
government efficiency, but it is not clear that they will actually cut
costs. Budget cuts are certain to be part of the solution to the problem,
but if revenues fail to grow in proportion to the economy, budget cuts
would have to occur annually. It is not clear that voters are ready to
accept the continued reduction in public services that this policy
implies.

During the last several years the erosion of state tax bases has
become obvious to more and more states. States have, however, limited
the crises by balancing their budgets on a year-by-year basis without
budget cutting, shifting spending to future years, and increasing tax

rates. It is not at all clear, however, that these measures will suffice for the rest of the decade.

The end of the recession has brought states some relief, but fiscal conditions are not likely to recover in the 1990s with the strength witnessed after most previous recessions. The serious structural issues of equity, sufficiency, and responsiveness will not be corrected by a stronger economic recovery.

In order to focus on the relationship between economic change and the deterioration of major state tax bases, this report excludes discussion of these important related topics:

• State and local government use of excise taxes and fees or charges for services

• State budget reform

We exclude the first topic because it has been widely addressed already, and because the way that the bases for excise taxes, fees, and charges fail to grow in proportion to the economy is already well known to legislators. We exclude the issue of state budget reform because another report of the length of this one would be required to do justice to the subject.

Not only is the current situation difficult, but fundamental economic and demographic changes in the 1990s will pose new difficulties for state revenue systems. In addition, there may be a fundamental shift in fiscal federalism brought by changes in federal tax policy, federal health care policy, or by a balanced-budget amendment to the federal constitution. If the federal government enacts additional tax increases to pay for health care or to reduce the annual deficit, it is likely to intrude further upon state tax bases. If the federal government continues to reassign domestic policy responsibility to the states, state tax systems will be stressed further. Significant change seems unavoidable. Because state revenue systems are already working poorly, it will be important to address existing structural inefficiencies as well as consider the effects of a changing environment.

Most state tax systems need to be redesigned to reflect the economic and demographic changes that are currently taking place in most states. These structural changes are expected to accelerate as the U. S. economy becomes increasingly global, service-oriented, and information-based. These changes, the slower economic growth projected for the decade of the 1990s, and the fact that state spending is increasing as a share of personal income will further complicate state fiscal conditions. As opposed to making incremental changes on a year-to-year basis, states should consider the following: evaluate the current and future state economic and demographic trends that will affect state revenues; redesign state tax systems to minimize the erosion of tax bases while increasing or maintaining equity, accountability, competitiveness, and administrative ease, and ease of compliance; cooperate with other states in revising tax systems to accommodate interstate and international changes; develop a uniform state response to federal intrusion and pre-emption of state tax bases.

SECTION 1
THE APPROACHING CRISIS
CHAPTER 1
FINANCING STATE GOVERNMENT IN THE 1990S

This study shows what's wrong with state taxes. It documents current problems, looks at state taxes in the light of the principles of a quality state tax system, and discusses some ways the problems could be addressed. The organizations that have sponsored this report hope that it will help governors, legislators, and voters throughout the nation understand and solve the structural tax problems the states face.

The pressure to change state tax systems is evidence that they suffer from significant problems. Such pressure has steadily increased over the last 20 years. There are many symptoms, some of them highly visible. California's Proposition 13 in 1978 was the first in a series of voter-initiated measures to reform tax systems, and constitutional amendments adopted in Colorado and Oklahoma in 1992 to require voter approval of tax increases are only the most recent. Legislatures and governors have also attempted major tax revisions, sometimes with success, as in the case of Connecticut's adoption of a broad-based personal income tax in 1991, and sometimes unsuccessfully, as when Florida and Massachusetts attempted to expand their state sales taxes to a wide range of services.

Other signs of discontent with existing state tax systems have received less attention—the numerous state tax studies of recent years, the somewhat increased use of taxes dedicated to specific expenditure purposes, and the erosion of the states' control of their traditional revenue sources through federal court decisions and federal pre-emption of state tax laws.

This report contends that such activity is evidence of the growing obsolescence of state tax systems. Voters' revolt against the property tax has been driven by a perception of unfair burdens. As this report demonstrates, a strong case can be made that state tax systems are in fact increasingly inequitable. State personal income taxes, general sales taxes, and business taxes have come to burden some kinds of personal income, some kinds of consumer and business purchases, and some kinds of business organizations and activities more heavily than others. In certain cases these inequities result from explicit policy decisions, but in many cases inequities result from changes in the American population and economy, ways of doing business, and consumer preferences which tax law has failed to take fully into consideration.

Inequities in tax policy have serious consequences. They can produce discontent among the voters that sometimes produces drastic solutions like Colorado's mandatory referral of all tax increases to the voters. Business taxes that weigh differently on different kinds of enterprises alter business investment decisions and weaken the competitive position of some businesses. Inequities can lead to efforts to carve out exemptions or exceptions, making inequities worse by providing favored treatment for some taxpayers. Inequities can lead to requests for Congress to intervene between states and taxpayers, on the grounds that states cannot provide fair and equitable treatment.

This study is designed as a practical discussion of the relationship of economic change and state tax policy for governors and legislators, many of whom are likely to grapple with the issues discussed here in the coming months and years. The purpose of this study is to document problems that exist with the structure of major state taxes, to analyze those problems in the context of the principles of a high-quality state tax system, and to discuss possible ways of resolving the problems.

The basic design of the tax systems with which states have entered the 1990s dates to the 1930s. They were designed for a nation of smokestack industries that was sunk in deep depression. In a nation whose economic nature has changed in ways and to an extent that could not have been imagined in the 1930s, state tax systems are far from being as efficient and equitable as they could be.[1]

Frequent changes in tax law have characterized the states recently. In the 1990 legislative sessions, 31 states enacted notable increases or decreases in their tax codes; 41 did so in 1991, as did 40 in 1992. Much of this change has affected the three major state taxes—the general sales tax, the personal income tax, and the corporate income tax.[2] Much of it has been ad hoc, driven not so much by considerations of long-term policy as by immediate revenue needs or particular interests and issues.

States have tended to overlook the need for fundamental tax reform while the national economy has changed. State tax systems have been revised, updated, and reformed to an extent that would be admirable if the American economy were still what it was in 1972. But it is not. Fundamental economic and demographic changes have changed the nature of tax bases and undermined state tax systems.

The economic changes are familiar. Heavy manufacturing is in relative decline, and growth in the economy springs from technologies, processes, and services that either did not exist or were far less significant 60 or even

20 years ago. Business activity is increasingly interstate and international in character, with even relatively small firms carrying on their activities across state and national borders. (The recent trade pact with Canada and the North American Free Trade Agreement reflect the trend, rather than point a new direction.) Communications technology is fundamentally reshaping almost every aspect of economic activity. Individual consumption patterns increasingly favor services over goods. Business taxes and sales taxes remain designed for outdated kinds of business structures and consumption patterns, reducing the taxes' equity and efficiency. In general, older, more settled kinds of economic activity are taxed more heavily than newer, dynamic kinds of activity.

The changes in demographic patterns are less familiar and their impact is less certain. But it appears that the aging of the American population, the growing share of wealth held by the elderly, migration and commuting patterns within the country, and present patterns of income distribution interact with state tax policy to shift the tax burden to the shrinking proportion of the population that is actively employed and lives in the state where its income arises.

The failure of state tax policy to respond adequately to such economic and demographic changes has kept state tax bases from growing in proportion to the growth of the national economy. Rate increases have provided growth in tax collections as a share of gross national product. But rate increases are not an adequate response. A state that responds to relative shrinkage in its sales tax base with rate increases (as consumers spend more of their disposable income on services) may find itself dependent on undesirably high rates, encouraging more consumption of services at the expense of goods, or facing tax evasion. State corporate income tax rates that are significantly higher than those in a neighboring state are often seen as producing an unfavorable business climate. Growth in personal income tax rates discriminates in favor of those whose income is sheltered. Thus efforts to deal piecemeal with the consequences of structural problems in state tax systems can make the problems worse, as this report demonstrates at length in section 2.

This is an appropriate time to release this report. Recovery from the recession is easing the extreme fiscal pressure that state governments experienced in 1991 and 1992, allowing decision makers to turn their attention from month-to-month survival to larger issues. Domestic issues are likely to seize more attention than they have over the past decade, due to changes on the international scene and increased concern for health care policy and long-term national economic growth. Attention to domestic policy is likely to generate more responsibilities for state governments, and those in turn will strain state revenue systems.

An assumption that underlies this report is that states need to address the structural problems in state tax systems regardless of the levels of taxation and of expenditures that a state finds appropriate. Spending cuts do not address the fundamental issues that this report identifies. Continuing demographic and economic change in the United States has made state tax systems less and less equitable and efficient. Without rate increases, revenues will not sustain any given level of expenditure over time because structural problems will prevent revenues from growing in proportion to the national economy. State tax systems are inefficient in reaching the growth in income and economic activity in the United States. (The discussion in the box explains this point in more detail.)

Even if voters were to decide that they wanted their state government to reduce its activity and spending steadily over time, it would be necessary to attend to the issues of equity, efficiency, and tax bases that this report discusses. Reductions in spending cannot address the deterioration of state tax bases and state tax systems' inequities and inefficiencies.

Making Revenue and Expenditure Growth Match

Suppose there was a consensus in a state that spending from its own sources (that is, leaving federal aid out of the picture) should grow at a rate equal to the combined rate of growth of the state economy and state population—a growth limit that some states have written into their constitutions. In order to fund such a "steady-state" budget, revenues would have to grow at the same rate. Most state taxes would not do so in the absence of rate increases. State sales taxes, which make up about one-third of total state tax collections, failed to grow as fast as personal income (a good proxy for state economic growth) in half the states from 1977 through 1990. The evidence is that, in the nation at large, the sales tax's responsiveness to economic growth is steadily weakening as consumer preferences shift from the purchase of goods to the purchase of services. Motor fuel taxes, in the absence of rate increases, grew as fast as the state economy in only five states from 1977 through 1990.[3] Personal income taxes can be structured more readily than other taxes to respond to economic growth, but since 1986 most changes in state personal income taxes have reduced their responsiveness to economic growth. If structural problems prevent state tax revenues from growing in proportion to economic and population growth, the state would either have to cut spending repeatedly or raise tax rates to sustain spending in proportion to such growth.

Notes

1. The meaning of efficiency and equity in relation to a state revenue system is discussed in chapter 3 of this report, "Keys to a Quality State Revenue System."

2. Corina Eckl, et al., *State Budget and Tax Actions 1990* (Denver, Colo: National Conference of State Legislatures, 1990), p. 16; *State Budget and Tax Actions 1991*, (Denver, Colo: National Conference of State Legislatures, 1991), p. 17; *State Tax Actions 1992* (Denver, Colo: National Conference of State Legislatures, 1992), p. 3.

3. Doug Olberding, "Taxes to Grow With," *State Government News* 36, no. 2 (February 1993): 11-14, citing recent work by Merl Hackbart for the Council of State Governments.

Chapter 2
Sources of State Revenue

This chapter is an overview of the sources of state revenues along with a brief discussion of how state revenues fit into the total of federal, state, and local revenues in the United States. It is concerned with 50-state totals. Details and comparisons of individual state revenue patterns are readily available in the annual publication *Significant Features of Fiscal Federalism* from the U.S. Advisory Commission on Intergovernmental Relations.[1]

State taxes, the subject of this report, are the major source of state governments' revenues, but they make up a little less than 60 percent of the total. Most of the rest comes from federal aid to state governments, which made up almost 23 percent of state revenue in FY 1990 (see figure 1).

Figure 1
Sources of State Government Revenue in FY 1990

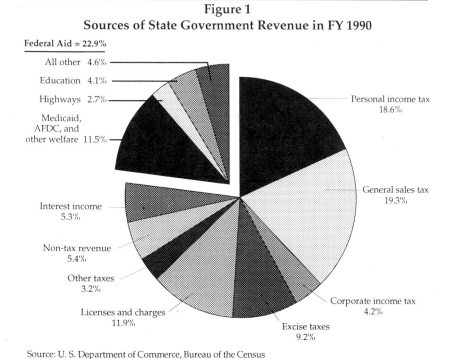

Federal Aid = 22.9%

All other 4.6%
Education 4.1%
Highways 2.7%
Medicaid, AFDC, and other welfare 11.5%
Interest income 5.3%
Non-tax revenue 5.4%
Other taxes 3.2%
Licenses and charges 11.9%
Excise taxes 9.2%
Corporate income tax 4.2%
General sales tax 19.3%
Personal income tax 18.6%

Source: U. S. Department of Commerce, Bureau of the Census

As figure 1 indicates, most state tax revenue comes from personal income and sales taxes. The third most important single tax is the corporate income tax, which in FY1990 produced 4.2 percent of state revenue compared to the more than 19 percent from general sales taxes. Excise taxes—mostly motor fuel, alcoholic beverage, and tobacco taxes—together are responsible for about twice as much annual state revenue as the corporate income tax.

Federal aid to state governments is a more important source of revenue than any single tax, at nearly 23 percent of the total. The purposes of federal aid are specified and outside state control. Half of federal payments to states are for welfare programs, principally Medicaid and AFDC. Other large chunks are earmarked for education and highways. The amount of federal aid that figure 1 shows as "all other" includes block grants that formerly were paid from the federal government to local governments, but are now pass-through money. States thus are little more than administrative arms of the federal government so far as this share of their budgets goes. Since many federal programs require matching funds from states' own resources—Medicaid is the most expensive example—federal policy influences or controls a larger share of state budgets than the amount of direct federal aid shown in figure 1 indicates.

The sources of state revenue have changed slowly over the past 20 years but the cumulative changes are significant. Figure 2 shows the origins of state revenue as a percentage of total state collections in FY 1970 and FY 1990. States have increasingly relied on personal income

Figure 2
Percentage Distribution of Major State Revenues, 1970 and 1990

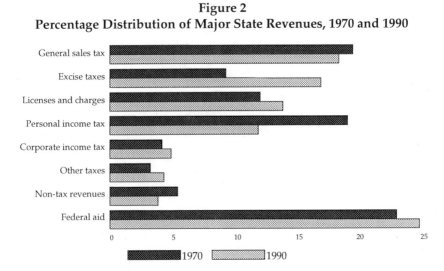

Source: U. S. Department of Commerce, Bureau of the Census

and general sales taxes. The amount of state revenue produced by personal income taxes grew from 11.8 percent in 1970 to 18.9 percent of the total in 1990. Some of the growth originated in the adoption of new income taxes in New Jersey, Ohio, Pennsylvania, and Rhode Island between 1971 and 1976: these four states are responsible for about 10 percent of all state income tax collections. General sales taxes have also grown in importance, but less rapidly than income taxes and, as explained later in this report, many rate increases have been needed to provide the small amount of growth indicated.

The shift to personal income taxes and to a smaller extent to general sales taxes has occurred in part because other traditional taxes have narrow bases and their structure can prevent them from producing revenues that keep up with growth in inflation in the absence of rate increases. That has been true of motor fuel and other excise taxes because as a rule they are based on the volume of a product sold rather than its value. In addition, as automobiles use less fuel per mile and as Americans consume less alcohol and tobacco per capita, excise taxes collected on sales of those products have shown even less growth.

State revenue has grown as a share of gross national product (GNP) over the past 20 years, although growth has not been steady. Much of the growth in state taxes as a percent of GNP occurred before 1985, as figure 3 shows; the shares of state revenue that originate in federal aid and in non-tax sources have also been fairly steady since 1985. Figure 3 clearly shows the impact of the back-to-back recessions of the early 1980s on state tax collections—first a decline, and then recovery as the tax increases enacted in response to the recession acted upon rapid national economic recovery.

Figure 3
State Revenue as a Percentage of Gross National Product, 1970-1990

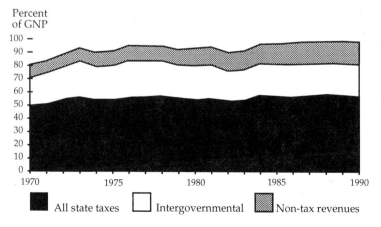

Source: U. S. Department of Commerce, Bureau of the Census

Federal aid followed a similar pattern of reduction and recovery at the time.

State Revenues in the National Context

Federal, state, and local governments differ greatly in their sources of revenue. Table 1 shows the principal sources of revenue for federal, state, and local governments. Two major differences between federal and state finance are of particular significance. One is the large income of federal insurance and pension funds—$371 billion in FY1990, 97 percent of which came from the payroll taxes for Social Security and Medicare. State and local governments collect nothing exactly like these taxes. Insurance and pension fund income for state and local governments consists of employer and employee payments to pension funds, workers' compensation funds, and unemployment funds plus those funds' investment earnings, which are added to the funds for their restricted purposes. While that is true for federal Medicare and Social Security taxes in a strict sense, in a more general sense the federal payroll taxes have substituted for general tax increases in recent years.

Another major difference in federal, state, and local finance is the role of external borrowing (which excludes borrowing from such internal federal sources as the Social Security trust fund). External borrowing accounted for about 23 percent of federal receipts in FY1990 but only 3.5 percent of state receipts and 6.3 percent of local government receipts. Federal payroll taxes and borrowing for continuing operations

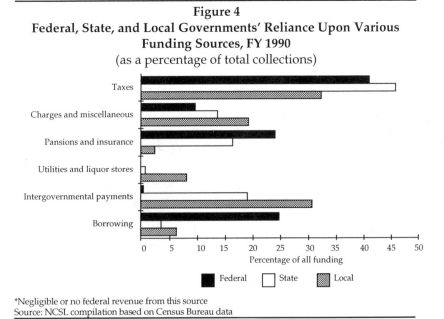

Figure 4
Federal, State, and Local Governments' Reliance Upon Various Funding Sources, FY 1990
(as a percentage of total collections)

*Negligible or no federal revenue from this source
Source: NCSL compilation based on Census Bureau data

supplement other federal revenue sources, as intergovernmental aid does for state and local governments. Figure 4 depicts the data in table 1.

Table 1
Categories and Amounts of Government Revenue
in the United States, FY 1990
(millions of dollars)

	Federal	State	Local
General revenue			
Intergovernmental	$ 2,911	$ 126,329	$ 190,723
Taxes	632,267	300,489	201,130
Other general revenue	148,212	90,612	120,489
Total, general revenue	**783,390**	**517,430**	**512,342**
Special-purpose revenue			
Insurance and pension funds	371,206	108,530	15,441
Utilities and liquor stores	0	6,213	52,430(a)
Total, continuing collections	**1,154,596**	**632,173**	**580,213**
External Borrowing	**265,896(b)**	**22,754**	**39,475**
Total, all receipts	**$ 1,140,492**	**$ 654,927**	**$ 619,688**

(a) Largely revenue of public utility authorities or special districts.
(b) Additional federal borrowing comes from internal sources like the Social Security trust fund.
Source: U. S. Department of Commerce, Bureau of the Census

A third important point is the traditional division of sources of tax revenue among the federal, state, and local governments (see figure 5). The federal government does not collect property taxes, and state governments have almost entirely resigned them to local governments. Although state governments have increasingly allowed local-option use of sales and excise taxes, they remain predominantly state government taxes. States collect more revenue from the general sales tax than from any other tax (45 states have general sales taxes). When the state revenue from excise taxes is added to general sales taxes, the states' reliance on consumption taxes is clear. Personal income taxes are shared between the federal government and states, 41 of which have broad-based personal income taxes, but when Social Security taxes are added to federal collections (as they are in figure 5), they dwarf those of the states. The nearly equal importance of general sales and personal income taxes to state revenue collections explains why state governments need to be concerned about the bases and productivity of both of those taxes.

Figure 5
Federal, State, and Local Governments'
Percentage Reliance Upon Taxes, 1990

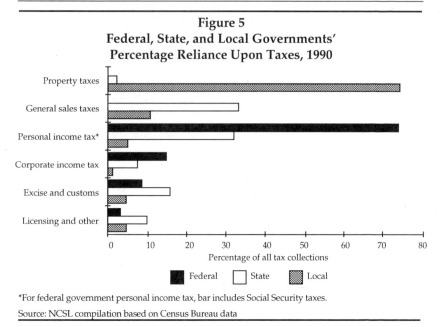

*For federal government personal income tax, bar includes Social Security taxes.

Source: NCSL compilation based on Census Bureau data

Revenue Collections as a Share of Gross National Product

Governmental revenue collections have represented a growing share of GNP over the past 20 years. The increase has occurred at all three levels of government (see table 2). The federal government's share of GNP has grown in the past decade because of increased payroll taxes for Social Security and Medicare; other federal tax collections now represent a smaller share of GNP than in 1980 or in 1970. Local governments' collections also have grown, though at a slower rate overall because of the property tax revolt of the late 1970s and early 1980s. Recent growth reflects the rising property values of the late 1980s. State collections have grown throughout the period, from 6 percent of GNP in 1970 to 7.5 percent in 1990.

Two sets of circumstances give some perspective to the growth in the share of GNP taken by state revenues. One is the long-term tendency for state governments to increase aid to local governments, especially for education. In that light, the growth in state revenue collections has been the counterpart of slower growth in local governments' collections. This trend may have peaked; state governments in 1991 and 1992 tended to reduce aid to local governments, a reflection of the budget difficulties caused by the recession and slow national recovery. The second circumstance is the federal government's reduced emphasis on domestic policy in the 1980s, other than spending on income-support and health programs like Medicare, Social Security, and Medicaid. State governments have picked up some of the slack; as noted above, in the period covered in table 2, state aid to local governments tended to increase. It may be significant that the sum of state and federal revenue collections, excluding OASDHI, changed little from 1970 to 1990. The total came to 23 percent of GNP in 1970, 23.3 percent in 1980, and 22.4 percent in 1990. To some extent, state revenue growth as a percent of GNP represents the funding of responsibilities shifted from the federal government.

Table 2
Federal, State, and Local Government Revenue Collections
As a Percentage of Gross National Product, 1970-1990
(excludes intergovernmental grants-in-aid)

Fiscal Year	Federal excluding OASDHI	Federal including OASDHI	State	Local
1970	17.0	21.3	6.0	5.3
1975	15.1	20.5	6.6	5.7
1980	16.6	22.2	6.7	5.2
1985	14.8	21.1	7.3	5.7
1990	14.9	21.8	7.5	6.1

Note: OASDHI (Old Age, Survivors, Disability, Health Insurance) refers to Medicare and Social Security tax collections.
Source: NCSL compilation based on Census Bureau data

Note

1. Data in this chapter are taken from the U. S. Department of Commerce, Bureau of the Census annual publications *Government Finances* and *State Governmental Finances*. Tables and graphs are compilations of data from those sources by staff of the National Conference of State Legislatures.

CHAPTER 3
KEYS TO A QUALITY TAX SYSTEM

Underlying all the diversity in state tax systems are principles of good tax policy that are consistently recognized in "blue ribbon" studies of state taxes, in economics and public administration, and in statements of groups of state officials such as *Principles Of A High-Quality State Revenue System*. These principles can be captured in five phrases. State tax systems should: (1) provide appropriate and timely revenues, (2) distribute burdens equitably, (3) promote economic efficiency and growth, (4) be easily administered, and (5) ensure accountability.

The principles are appropriate for the combination of taxes levied by states alone, taxes shared with local government, and the local tax choices controlled by state law. Together, these constitute a state's tax system. A tax with volatile revenues or inequitable burdens is not necessarily objectionable if other state or local taxes offset its effects. Besides considerations of fairness and economic impact, other reasons to consider state and local taxes as a package are the possibilities of reducing the costs of compliance and administration by making tax bases identical and by consolidating administration.

A State Tax System Should Provide Appropriate and Timely Revenues

The purpose of a tax system is to raise revenue to provide public services. Determining the level of services is a political process in which elected representatives weigh the desirability of private versus public spending and choose among competing demands for public resources. The tax system should fund these decisions, but not determine them.

The tax system should provide adequate revenues to cover budgeted outlays. Revenues should be certain and stable enough that spending can be based on them without sudden changes dictated by revenue surprises. To avoid such changes, the tax system must be supplemented by careful estimating of revenues and spending, and hedges against adversity such as budget stabilization funds and making some spending contingent on revenue availability. Stability promotes efficiency in the private sector by giving citizens greater certainty about the services government will provide and the taxes they will have to pay.

Tax systems are most likely to distort spending decisions when, over time, the revenues generated from existing tax laws deviate significantly from the costs of maintaining current services. Faster automatic revenue growth will permit state and local governments to take an ever-increasing share of personal income. Slower revenue growth will constantly force difficult choices between service cuts and tax increases.

Overall revenue growth should approximate the impact of inflation and population growth on spending needs and taxpayers' ability to pay. If revenue growth also captures a share of national productivity growth, a stable tax system will hold the share of personal income taken in taxes nearly constant, reserving to elected officials the decisions over whether this share should be increased or reduced.

Most state tax systems seek balance to ensure stable revenues and to avoid such a concentration of tax burdens on a few sources as to make rates distort economic behavior. Balance means the use of many different tax bases. Balance also requires that taxes be broad-based with a minimum of exclusions and deductions. This allows lower rates, and thus less distortion of economically efficient decisions, and makes revenues less volatile. Balance and broad bases make it easier for state officials to adjust taxes in small increments with minimal economic and administrative disturbance.

A State Tax System Should Distribute Burdens Equitably

Most people agree that fairness requires that taxpayers in similar situations be treated similarly—firms as well as households—and that taxes should be related to the ability to pay. The perception of fairness is almost as important as fairness itself. Taxpayers must believe that the tax system does not benefit some groups or individuals at the expense of others. Business taxpayers must believe that the tax system creates a level playing field.

Reaching those goals is complicated by the lack of agreement on how to measure either firms' or individuals' relative ability to pay taxes. A tax clearly related to one measurement of ability to pay, such as value of property holdings, may appear unrelated to some other measurement, such as annual income or consumer spending. One criterion is *proportionality*, which means taking an equal percentage of the income (or other tax base) of taxpayers whose incomes are different. The state tax systems of most states are *regressive*, that is, the proportion of income taken as taxes is lower for higher income households. Few, if any, state tax systems are *progressive*, which is to say they take a larger share of the income of higher-income people than of lower-income people. Those like Vermont and California, which rely heavily on personal income taxes, can approach progressivity.

Judgments of regressivity or progressivity should be applied to state and local tax systems as a whole, not to particular taxes and user charges. Since state sales and excise taxes tend by their nature to be regressive, they would have to play a much smaller role in state tax policy if proportionality or progressivity became a requirement for all state tax revenue sources. There are ways to handle extreme cases when fairness on one dimension may indicate unfairness on another. One such device is the circuitbreakers used to provide relief to those whose property taxes are an extreme percentage of their income. State officials should, at a minimum, have knowledge of the likely effects of tax policy decisions on taxpayers of varying incomes and wealth.

When taxes are raised for specific programs, the distribution of new benefits sometimes can be related to the distribution of new tax burdens. Under some circumstances, it may be appropriate to allocate tax burdens in rough proportion to benefits received. Although gasoline excise taxes are regressive, the issue is rarely raised because their use for highway construction and maintenance is regarded as justification. Sales taxes are regressive, but using sales tax revenues to finance programs which benefit lower-income people somewhat compensates for the unequal tax burden in a way that using sales tax revenues for benefits for upper-income people would not.

A State Tax System Should Promote Economic Efficiency And Growth
The general rule is that taxes should be neutral in their effect upon behavior. Taxes should not affect a consumer's choice between two products, or between a product and a service, or the choice of one production technique over another. This is a strong argument for spreading the tax burden over many tax bases with few exemptions, deductions, and other special provisions so that the distorting effects, though inevitable, remain small.

The impact of taxes on state and national economic growth is an important tax policy consideration, usually focusing on the competitiveness of a state with other states. In considering taxes on firms, the concern is to avoid tax burdens that significantly exceed those of other states and nations. In considering taxes on individuals, the usual concern is over differential burdens so significant that they would cause households to move from, or avoid locating in, a state or to shop across state borders. Whether particular current or proposed taxes have such impacts are questions that can be answered by research. The answers vary with each state and circumstance.

On the other hand, tax policy is sometimes an appropriate tool for encouraging or discouraging behavior, when market forces, regulation, or outright prohibition are inadequate or ineffective in reaching some policy goal. So, taxes are sometimes used to discourage activity, such as creating pollution or smoking, where prohibition is impractical or deemed undesirable. Unlike prohibition, taxes preserve a degree of freedom of choice and can enable states to recover a portion of the social costs the activity causes.

Taxes are usually more effective in discouraging activities than in encouraging them because taxes are inherently a negative tool: they take away resources and income. Tax incentives are inefficient because a large proportion of the tax savings go to people and businesses for doing what they would have done in any case. Unlike direct outlays, the costs of tax expenditures tend to be invisible and to grow without review.

A State Tax System Should Be Easily Administered
Ease of administration, sometimes called simplicity, encompasses several closely related principles:

• Minimizing costs to the collecting government (administrative cost) and to the taxpayer (compliance cost).

• Improving enforcement and preventing evasion.

• Reinforcing confidence in the tax system.

Complexity in the tax system encourages special provisions that erode fairness and lower confidence in tax systems and the elected officials who created them. Simplicity makes it easy for taxpayers to comply with the law, for businesses to plan, for the state to administer, and for citizens to understand the system so that they know that others are also paying their fair share.

A State Tax System Should Ensure Accountability
There is no agreement among state officials on whether government should shrink or expand relative to the private sector, but there is agreement that such decisions should be explicit—with choices openly arrived at in full view of the electorate—rather than being hidden in obscure features of state tax systems. Accountability suggests linking responsibilities for spending and raising revenues and avoiding hidden tax preferences for favored firms or groups of individuals.

Accountability also links responsibility for raising revenue to credit for spending it. Local governments should raise the funds for local expenditures, with state governments making suitable allowances for the size of local tax bases. State governments should avoid unfunded mandates on local governments. Doing this requires that state officials afford local officials considerable flexibility in tax policy.

Many different mechanisms can encourage accountability. Some states favor sunset concepts for taxes, such as temporary levies and automatic expiration of tax expenditures. Others favor periodic reporting of tax provisions creating exceptions for designated groups (tax expenditure reports) and/or periodic assessments of tax policy overall or its impact on groups of different incomes or geographic location.

SECTION 2
PROBLEMS WITH STATE REVENUE SYSTEMS

S ection 2 focuses on the problems with state revenue systems, analyzing the ways that state tax systems have been affected by changes in production and consumption patterns, ways of doing business, the age distribution of the population, the distribution of income, and competition among states for economic development. Section 2 also discusses two subjects of a different sort that have enormous significance for state tax policies: federal pre-emption of state taxing authority and the long-term decline of the relative importance of the property tax as a source of state and local government revenue.

The primary theme of this section is that state tax systems have serious structural problems—problems, that is, that result from state taxes having been designed for other circumstances than those now prevailing. The secondary theme is that interstate competition, despite some advantageous effects, makes the structural problems of state taxes worse.

Section 2 mostly takes up issues of general sales taxes, personal income taxes, and corporate income taxes because among them they produce 72 percent of state tax revenue and because the way they are affected by economic change and changes in consumption patterns has not received adequate attention. Local property taxes come into the discussion because the long term trend of reduced reliance on property taxes in financing local services is a major component of the changing environment in which state tax systems operate.

CHAPTER 4
ECONOMY, POPULATION, AND INCOME

The problem: The economy, the population, and the distribution of income in the United States have changed over the past twenty years in ways that have reduced the responsiveness of many existing state taxes to growth in the national economy.

Economic activity in the United States is steadily shifting away from the production of tangible goods to services. Figure 6 shows the dramatic shift. It measures major sectors in the American economy as a component of Gross National Product (GNP). In the 1930s, services accounted for about one-third of GNP. However, after World War II, the service sector began to grow as a share of total economic output; it now accounts for over 52 percent of GNP. As figure 6 shows, the share of national output attributed to production of tangible goods has declined steadily. By 1975, the production of services contributed more to the national economy than the production of tangible goods.

Figure 6
Services and Tangible Goods in the National Economy
as a Percentage of GNP, 1940-1990

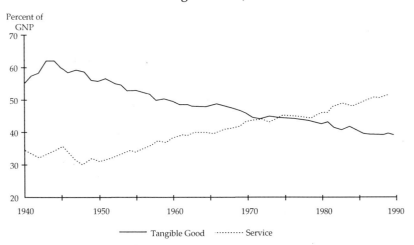

Source: Federation of Tax Administrators compilation based on Bureau of Economic Analysis data

The service sector has been the fastest growing sector of the U.S. economy in recent years. The annual growth rates of earnings in the major sectors of the American economy other than agriculture appear in table 3. Earnings in the goods-producing sector stagnated during the 1980s, as the table shows, with the annual real growth rate slowing to only 0.2 percent. Meanwhile, the services sector saw inflation-adjusted growth rates averaging 3.8 percent a year. Health services saw the fastest rate of growth in earnings, increasing at a real annual rate of 6.1 percent. This was followed by business services at 6 percent. Income from consumer services grew by 4.6 percent, which also exceeds the 2.7 percent for total nonagricultural earnings.[1]

Table 3
Annual Growth Rates in Real Earnings by Industry
(Percent growth over previous year)

	1975-80	1980-90
Total Nonagricultural Earnings	3.4%	2.7%
Goods Producing Sectors	3.9	0.2
Mining	7.8	-3.6
Construction	4.4	1.4
Total Manufacturing	3.5	0.1
Nondurable Goods	2.5	0.8
Durable Goods	4.1	-0.3
Service Producing Sectors	3.1	3.8
Transportation & Utilities	3.7	1.3
Wholesale Trade	3.8	2.1
Retail Trade	1.7	2.0
Consumer Services	3.8	4.6
Lodging/Amusement	4.4	5.4
Producer Services	5.8	3.8
Finance, Insurance, Real Estate	4.4	4.7
Business Services	9.7	6.0
Health & Human Services	4.1	5.9
Health Services	5.1	6.1
Educational Services	-1.2	4.7
Government	0.9	2.8

Source: Compiled by William Duncombe from Bureau of Economic Analysis data

The shift in national production and consumption from goods to services has profound consequences for all major state taxes. The base of the most important source of state tax revenue, the general sales tax, is largely the purchase of tangible goods. As consumption shifts from goods to services, sales tax collections fail to grow in proportion to the growth in the national economy unless rates are repeatedly raised.[2]

The second largest source of state tax revenue, the personal income tax, can be affected by the shift from production of goods to services if service jobs fail to pay as much as the manufacturing jobs they replace. For example, Michigan lost 170,000 manufacturing jobs from 1979 through 1988 and gained 199,000 service jobs as replacements. But 80 percent of the manufacturing jobs had paid more than $34,000 a year; only 5 percent of the service jobs do so and 60 percent pay less than $17,200.[3]

Another important source of state tax revenue, the corporate income tax, is affected in a different way by this shift. States' rules for dividing the income of multistate service corporations (for tax purposes) among the states in which they operate now appear unable to produce a fair division or one that can readily be enforced. The issues will be examined in detail in chapters 6 and 7 of this report.

Changes in the Population

The national trend toward an older population will continue well into the following century, as figure 7 indicates. In 1960, slightly more than 9 percent of Americans were over age 65. Currently the percentage is approaching 13 percent, where it will remain throughout this decade before resuming a rapid increase after the turn of the century.

A few states, but not the nation at large, will simultaneously experience growth in the proportion of the population under 18. In California, for example, the working-age population (18 to 65) is expected to fall significantly in proportion to the dependent population (those under 18 or over 65) from 1990 to the turn of the century.

Such changes raise issues of the equity and adequacy of state taxes because personal income and consumption taxes rest primarily upon the working-age population.[4] Even though people over 65 are less likely than other Americans to fall below the poverty line, their average income is only about half that of Americans between ages 24 and 65.[5] In addition, state and federal policy tends to grant favorable tax treatment to the elderly. Relatively low incomes among the elderly population are a reason for their favorable tax treatment; little attention has been given to the question of the impact such treatment has on tax collections overall and the shift of tax burdens to the working-age population.

Figure 7
Percentage of the U.S. Population Over Age 65, 1960-2020

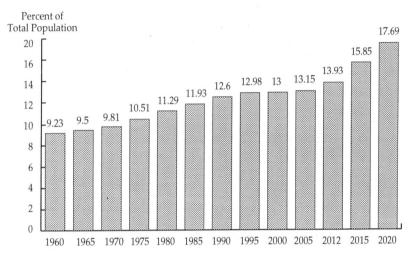

Note: Figures for 1995-2020 are projected

Source: Bureau of the Census

The combination of an aging population with its reduced incomes and favorable tax treatment can be significant for state tax collections. In Arizona, for example, where the population over 65 has grown somewhat faster than in the United States overall, the Legislature's Joint Budget Committee staff observed in 1992.

Another facet of lagging revenues was the growth in the elderly population. The elderly enjoyed a significantly favorable income tax treatment relative to other age groups; therefore their state tax payments grew less than their income. Meanwhile, income growth from all other groups who pay a higher share of income taxes was too anemic to make up the shortfall.[6]

The aging of the American population may affect sales taxes through changes in patterns of consumption. Age itself seems to have an effect on consumption patterns, as William Duncombe suggests:

Retired households are more apt to consume medical care, food at home and utilities, and less apt to spend on restaurants, entertainment, and household services. The relative growth in the elderly population will probably dampen sales tax growth [in states where] food, health care, and utilities are generally not taxable.[7]

As a larger proportion of the population falls into this category, the sales tax base may shrink in proportion to national personal income.

The Shift Away from Taxable Income

Changes in the nature of personal income in the United States are reducing the share of income that is subject to state personal income taxes. Earnings are falling as a proportion of national personal income. A growing proportion of national personal income takes the forms of transfer payments like Social Security and Aid to Families with Dependent Children and employer payments for non-taxable employee benefits. Table 4 summarizes the change.

Table 4
Sources of National Personal Income, 1970-1990

Year	Total Personal Income ($ Millions)	Net Earnings	Percentage of Total Personal Income		
			Dividends, Interest, and Rent	Other Labor Income	Transfer Payments
1970	825,534	72.4%	13.3%	3.9%	10.4%
1975	1,308,462	67.6	12.6	5.0	14.8
1980	2,254,076	64.7	14.7	6.1	14.5
1985	3,317,545	62.5	17.1	5.6	14.8
1990	4,662,698	62.1	17.4	5.5	15.0

Note: Net earnings include wages, salaries, and proprietors' income. Other labor income includes employer contributions for employee benefits.

Source: NCSL compilation from Department of Commerce data

Table 4 shows that net earnings—wages, salaries, and proprietors' income—fell from 72.4 percent of total personal income in 1970 to 62.1 percent in 1990. Income from dividends, interest, and rent, which generally is subject to taxation, did not grow fast enough to make up this loss. Transfer payments grew from 10.4 percent to 15 percent, and the category of other labor income—untaxed benefits—grew from 3.9 percent to 5.5 percent of personal income. The shift is important because (1) sales tax purchases tend to come from wages and salary income[8] and (2) transfer payments and other labor income are at least partially sheltered from income taxation.

Although some social security payments and pension benefits are subject to federal and state income tax, they receive favored treatment. States are especially likely to favor public employees' retirement benefits. Net earnings and investment return do not receive such favorable treatment. The consequence has been that state taxation increasingly bears upon wage-earners and those who receive income from investments, as explained in the box.

Conclusion

Changes in the national economy, in the shape of the American population, and in the distribution of American income have a direct bearing upon state tax policy. Such changes help determine who pays taxes and the amount of taxes people pay just as surely as the debates over tax policy that take place in state capitols and the media. The impacts of economic and demographic changes on state tax systems tend to go unnoticed. This report is intended to bring attention to such changes, analyze their consequences, and suggest ways that state tax policy can take such changes into account.

The Shifting Incidence of Income Taxes

Because the share of total personal income represented by net earnings and investment income fell from 85.7 percent in 1970 to 79.5 percent in 1990, the state tax burden measured against earnings and investment income has grown faster than tax collections as a share of total personal income, as table 5 shows. Measured against all personal income, state tax collections grew from $5.81 per $100 to $6.44 from 1970 to 1990, an increase of 11 percent over 20 years. Measured against the smaller, and shrinking, base of earnings and investment income, state collections grew from $6.78 per $100 in 1970 to $8.11 in 1990, an increase of just under 20 percent. These numbers somewhat overstate the case, since some transfer payments are subject to state income tax and are used in part for consumption subject to state sales and excise taxes. But they accurately indicate the direction of change and they reflect the perception by the working population that their tax burden is growing.

Table 5
State Tax Collections per $100 of Net Earnings and Investment Income, 1970-1990

Year	Earnings and Investment Income as a Percentage of Personal Income	State Tax Collections Per $100 of Income: On Earnings and Investment Income	Total Personal Income
1970	85.7%	$6.78	$5.81
1975	80.2%	$7.64	$6.12
1980	79.4%	$7.66	$6.08
1985	79.6%	$8.16	$6.49
1990	79.5%	$8.11	$6.44
		Up 20%	Up 11%

Source: NCSL compilation based on Department of Commerce data

Notes

1. William Duncombe, "Economic Change and the Evolving State Tax Structure: The Case of the Sales Tax" (paper delivered at Taxes and Spending in the Age of Deficits, A Symposium of the National Tax Association, Arlington, Virginia, May 1992), p. 117.

2. John Mikesell, "Sales Tax Policy in a Changing Economy: Balancing Political and Economic Logic Against Revenue Needs," *Public Budgeting and Finance* 12, no. 1 (Spring 1992): 88.

3. Warren C. Gregory, Solving Michigan's Budget Deficit: *Opportunity from Crisis*, (Lansing, Mich.: Michigan State House of Representatives Fiscal Agency, 1990), pp. 3-8.

4. For an excellent discussion of this issue, *see* Keith Carlson, "State Income Tax Treatment of Senior Citizens Changing," *State Tax Notes*, 2, no. 6 (February 10, 1992): 192-200.

5. U.S. Department of Commerce, Bureau of the Census, *Statistical Abstract of the United States*, 1992 (Washington, D.C.: U.S. Government Printing Office, 1992), Tables 697, 725-730.

6. Arizona State Legislature, Joint Legislative Budget Committee, "Demographics and the State Budget" in *Budget Status Report Issue 1992-1* (Phoenix, Ariz.: May 1992), pp 53-65.

7. William Duncombe, "Economic Change." Words in brackets added to original.

8. There is a useful discussion of this point in Gregory, "Michigan's Budget Deficit."

CHAPTER 5
INTERSTATE COMPETITION FOR ECONOMIC DEVELOPMENT

The problem: Interstate tax competition for economic development can undermine state tax bases, produce tax inequities, and inhibit tax policy reforms—at times without providing compensatory benefits.

Concessions designed to lure new businesses or stimulate economic development usually come to mind when people think of interstate tax competition. There are, however, other forms and levels of interstate competition.[1] Some may have desirable effects by promoting efficient, balanced tax systems. Other forms of competition are commonly seen as eroding the tax base and producing potential inequities without stimulating the development for which they were intended. From a longer term perspective, one of the more important impacts of interstate tax competition is the degree to which it inhibits states' efforts to modernize and update their tax systems.

States tend to define their tax system by reference to each other. They often take pains to design their tax systems to avoid being distinctly different from neighboring or competing states, particularly in ways that the business community dislikes. This form of interstate competition can promote balanced tax systems with broad bases and low marginal rates. It can also promote stability and certainty which are of paramount importance to businesses.

Traditionally it was believed that such competition would lead to anemic revenue production and a generally low level of public services as every state tried to provide a lower cost environment than its neighbors. More recently, state tax analysts have begun to argue that such competition can have a beneficial effect on state and local fiscal systems by encouraging states to provide services at the least cost.[2] They argue that mobile individuals and businesses will choose the government with the most preferable package of services and taxes. Such choices can promote more efficient government, while allowing for diversity in taxes and size of government.[3]

Every state uses targeted or general tax incentives to stimulate job creation and business location within the state.[4] Most often, states have enacted special tax credits, exemptions or deductions intended to promote activities like capital investment and job creation and to make a state more attractive for new businesses. Recently states have increased the use of special tax concessions for the benefit of particular large businesses seeking to relocate their headquarters or a major facility. These efforts can turn into bidding wars as states compete to provide tax concessions, infrastructure improvements, and other incentives.[5]

Research on the effectiveness of tax incentives has found mixed results. Some studies find that job creation or income growth are affected by state tax levels. Other studies find no significant relationship between state taxes and economic development and point out that many different factors influence business location decisions, most of which comprise a larger portion of a business's operating costs than state taxes.[6] Some of these factors are at least partially under the control of state government, like access to financing, the regulatory environment, quality of schools and universities, and quality of government services. There are important factors state government cannot control like the proximity to markets and suppliers, transportation costs and cost of utilities.[7] For the most part, such studies conclude that state incentives are unlikely to have a significant impact on business location decisions.

Both general and targeted tax concessions can cause serious problems for state tax systems. They erode the tax base, which diminishes revenue growth. Some states report substantial revenue losses from their business tax incentives, which must be made up through higher taxes elsewhere or reduced services.[8] To the extent that a state attempts to target its incentives in an effort to improve their stimulative effect, the administration of the incentive is likely to be made increasingly complex.[9] In addition, targeted concessions may mean higher taxes on industries or businesses which do not qualify for the incentive. This distorts the horizontal equity of the tax system by treating similar businesses differently. The recent bidding wars have involved only large businesses and facilities which raises questions of fairness and equity. Bidding wars also can breed public distrust of government and businesses, particularly if the actions of the recipient business do not coincide with public expectations.

Implications for Tax Law Revision
An invidious and often unrecognized impact of interstate competition is the chilling effect it has on state efforts to reform tax systems. State efforts to update their tax codes generally will extend the reach of state taxes to transactions or businesses not currently taxed, or at least will tax such activities in a different and possibly more complete fashion. Not surprisingly, some view such proposals as detrimental to the economic development and business climate of a state (which, given how little is certain about the impact of taxes on economic development, is a possibility). The perception makes revenue-neutral tax reform difficult,

particularly if other states have not undertaken similar reforms, and can inhibit cooperative efforts to improve uniformity and increase compliance with the tax laws.[10]

The result of states' efforts to broaden the sales tax to services demonstrates the effect of competition on attempts to modernize state tax policy. The impact on the tax climate and the concern that some businesses might move out of state have been common issues in such efforts. Indeed, the impact on business helped bring the repeal of Florida's and Massachusetts's expansion of the sales tax base to services.[11]

Conclusion

Some interstate tax competition is useful; some is detrimental. Some forms can lead to government services being delivered more efficiently. Other forms can inhibit modernization of state tax systems and erode the tax base.

Notes

1. *See* particularly, Daphne Kenyon, *Interjurisdictional Tax and Policy Competition: Good or Bad for the Federal System?* (Washington, D.C.: U.S. Advisory Commission on Intergovernmental Relations, April 1991) and Daphne Kenyon and John Kincaid, eds., *Competition Among States and Local Governments— Efficiency and Equity in American Federalism* (Washington, D.C.: The Urban Institute Press, 1991).

2. This analysis assumes that all government services are paid directly by a state's citizens through taxes. However, this relationship does not hold for some states that can export a portion of their tax burden. For most states, the ability to export taxes is limited.

3. *See* Kenyon, *Interjurisdictional Tax and Policy Competition*, and John Shannon, "Federalism's Invisible Regulator—Interjurisdictional Competition," in Kenyon and Kincaid, eds., *Competition Among States and Local Governments*.

4. A catalog of state business tax incentives exceeds 800 pages. National Association of State Development Agencies, *Incentives for Business Investment and Development in the U.S.*, 3rd ed. (Washington, D.C.: Urban Institute Press, 1991).

5. Some recent examples include United Airlines, Sears, Roebuck and Co., Northwest Airlines, General Dynamics, McDonnell-Douglas, and Air West.

6. For a comparison of a number of studies, *see* Kenyon, *Interjurisdictional Tax and Policy Competition*, pp. 31-46. Many studies have concluded that regional differences in labor costs, construction costs and energy costs are generally too large to be offset by differences in tax levels. *See* Cornia, Testa and Stocker, *State-Local Fiscal Incentives and Economic Development*, Urban and Regional Development Series No. 4 (Washington, D.C.: Academy for Contemporary Problems, 1978).

7. A summary of these factors is provided in Richard D. Pomp, "Reforming a State Corporate Income Tax," *Albany Law Review* 51, No. 3/4 (Spring/Summer 1987): 395-397. *See* also *Harley T. Duncan*, "Do State Taxes Affect Business Location Decisions?" (paper delivered to the California Tax Policy Conference, San Diego, California, November 1992), p. 5.

8. For example, West Virginia officials estimate that special tax credits cost the state nearly 4.5 percent of total general revenue tax collections. Mark Muchow, "The West Virginia Investment Tax Credit Experience" (paper presented to the 1992 Federation of Tax Administrators Revenue Estimating and Tax Research Conference, Cooperstown, New York, September 1992).

9. For further discussion, *see* Harley T. Duncan, "State Legislators and Tax Administrators: Can We Talk?," in Steven D. Gold, ed., *The Unfinished Agenda for State Tax Reform* (Denver, Colo.: National Conference of State Legislatures, 1988), pp. 83-99.

10. For a discussion of the "casualties of go-it-alone taxation," *see* Alice M. Rivlin, *Reviving the American Dream: The Economy, the States and the Federal Government* (Washington, D.C.: The Brookings Institution, 1992), pp. 137-142.

11. Other factors contributing to the repeal of these service taxes include not adequately addressing the pyramiding problem and the use tax on interstate transactions. These issues are discussed in more detail in chapter 14 of this report. For a discussion of the Florida experience, *see* James Francis, "The Florida Sales Tax on Services: What Really Went Wrong?" in Steven D. Gold, ed., *The Unfinished Agenda for State Tax Reform*, pp. 129-50.

CHAPTER 6
SHIFTING FROM MANUFACTURING TO SERVICES

The problem: State sales and corporate income taxes have not kept pace as the American economy has shifted from the production and consumption of goods to the production and consumption of services.

The shift in the U.S. economy toward greater production and consumption of services has had direct consequences for state tax systems. Sales and use taxes largely apply to retail transactions involving tangible personal property. Consequently, the proportion of untaxed retail transactions grows as the consumption of services increases. The growth of service industries creates problems associated with state corporate income taxes as well, such as determining where a business is subject to tax, and in dividing the income of service enterprises among the states in which they are doing business. Growth in service industries can also affect the property tax base in a state, depending upon how intangibles and personal property are taxed in comparison with real property.

State sales and use taxes and corporate income taxes were designed at a time when the production of goods was paramount in the American economy and their bases are linked to the production and consumption of goods in ways that have caused the bases to shrink relative to the size of the total economy as its focus has shifted. This section explains how that has happened. Chapter 13 offers suggestions for dealing with the problem.

Implications for Retail Sales Taxes

State and local retail sales taxes are a good example of how states have failed to adapt their tax systems to changes in the economy. Because more than half of the states enacted their current sales tax statutes during the 1930s, the tax base reflects the nature and condition of the U.S. economy during the Great Depression. Most personal consumption at that time consisted of purchases of tangible property. Such services as existed (other than housing, education, and utilities) were generally manual labor services. As a result, most sales tax systems became taxes on retail sales of tangible property; they largely exempted purchases of services by not including them within the scope of the tax.

Even today, 23 states exempt labor services from sales taxation. Despite recent attempts in some states to broaden the sales tax base, service transactions go largely untaxed in most states.[1] This causes tax collections to lag behind overall economic growth since the sales tax captures a declining share of a state's economic activity. The absence of services from the tax base erodes the vitality of the sales tax and confronts state officials with the prospect of increasing tax rates to maintain current levels of revenue.

The average state sales tax rate grew from 3.54 percent in 1970 to 5.07 percent in 1992. Yet due to the narrowing of the tax base through enacted exemptions and increased service consumption, the substantial rate increase succeeded only in holding state sales tax collections constant, when expressed as a share of GNP. State sales tax collections were 2.7 percent of GNP in 1970, and they remained at 2.7 percent of GNP in 1990.[2]

The shift in economic activity toward the service sector has had a direct impact on the sales tax base as shown in figure 8, which compares the proportion of personal consumption expenditures accounted for by various categories of goods and services in 1960 and 1990. The share of personal consumption spent on services (excluding housing services) has grown steadily since 1960, increasing from 26 percent in 1960 to 42 percent in 1991. On the other hand, purchases of tangible goods fell from about 60 percent to 44 percent of consumption. Purchases of tangible items other than food fell from 34 percent to 28 percent of total purchases.

Figure 8
The Changing Mix of Personal
Consumption Expenditures, 1960-1990

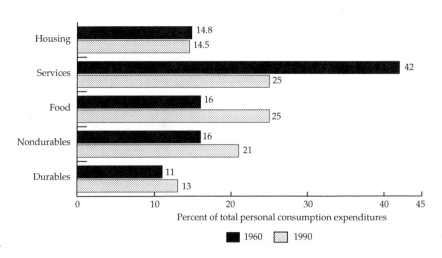

Percent of total personal consumption expenditures

■ 1960 ▨ 1990

Source: Federation of Tax Administrators

The growth in the service sector means that the traditional sales tax is applied to a smaller and smaller share of national economic activity. The revenue loss can be illustrated, if not measured exactly. In 1960, each percentage point of the sales tax rate in the states with sales taxes generated on average $6.90 per $1,000 of personal income. By 1990, this figure had dropped to $5.40 per $1,000 of personal income (a decrease of 20 percent). Based on total personal income in 1990 of $4.8 trillion, states would have generated an additional $36 billion in sales tax revenues if the productivity of the tax had remained at its 1960 level.[3] The National Association of State Budget Officers recently examined sales tax data from three states with widely different degrees of service taxation and found that the state with the broadest sales tax base saw sales tax collections from services grow relative to personal income while collections in the other states remained flat.[4]

Excluding services from state and local sales and use tax bases raises tax policy issues beyond that of revenue productivity. First, exclusion affects the neutrality of the tax by treating similar transactions in dissimilar fashion. A system that taxes the purchase of new items, but does not tax repairs, favors repairs over purchases. Exclusion of services will also affect the stability of the tax during the economic cycle. A tax structure that includes only purchases of tangible personal property (especially one that exempts food for home consumption) is more sensitive to downturns in the economy than a more broadly based tax. Finally, the expansion of a sales tax to services can make the sales tax less regressive.[5]

On the other hand, the difficulties involved in including certain services in the sales tax base have been serious enough to have caused two states to repeal the expansion of the sales tax to services soon after enactment, and have caused other states to move cautiously in expanding the sales tax to services. The problems include tax pyramiding if business services are included, collection of use tax on interstate transactions, and defining the services to be taxed. These and related issues are examined in section 3.[6]

Implications for Direct Business Taxation
The shift in the economic base from goods toward services also affects direct business taxation: the revenue yield from state business taxes, the impact of taxes on the relative competitiveness of in-state and out-of-state service businesses, and the division of the tax burden between service businesses and traditional manufacturing and mercantile businesses.

Many Service Businesses Are Not Subject to Direct Taxation

Finally, much of the production of services occurs in non-profit organizations and unincorporated businesses. Primary examples of the former are non-profit hospitals, nursing homes, cultural organizations like museums or ballet companies, and child care facilities. Examples of unincorporated businesses include personal service businesses operated as sole proprietorships, like dry cleaners, car repair shops, and small restaurants, and the professional service businesses often operated as partnerships, like legal, accounting, engineering, and architectural firms. A major segment of the commercial real estate industry operates in the legal form of the limited partnership.

As such businesses have come to make up a larger share of the national economic base, the tax base has shrunk because unincorporated businesses are not taxed directly. Instead, the business income is for tax purposes attributed to the owners of the businesses and is taxed as personal income.[7] The income of non-profits, of course, is not taxed at all. Thus, the concentration of much production of services in the nonprofit and unincorporated sectors means that the economic shift toward services is narrowing the corporate income tax base as well as the state sales tax base.

Traditional Interstate Tax Apportionment Has Shortcomings

With regard to the income of a multistate corporation, the traditional way of dividing or "apportioning" taxable income among states may not be appropriate for many service industries.

State apportionment rules treat the sale of goods as occurring at the point where the customer receives them (i.e., on a "destination basis"—see Glossary). This acknowledges the contribution of sales to profits and ensures that states which provide services that allow a market for an out-of-state corporation to operate are able to tax a share of its net income.[8] But sales of services, according to traditional apportionment rules, occur in the state in which the service is produced or performed ("origin basis").

The disparate treatment of sales of goods and services probably had little significance when it was adopted, because at the time most services were performed in the customer's vicinity. Cheap transportation and powerful telecommunications and data processing technologies now mean that any number of business services are sold across state lines—for example, design of an office building or preparation of a weekly payroll. Besides extending the markets of traditional service industries, technology has fostered entirely new ones in communications, finance, information and entertainment that can operate nationally from one location. Examples come readily to mind—satellites bouncing television shows into the most remote corners of Alaska, a national database like Lexis, and a regional bank that issues credit cards to customers in every state.

These changes mean that attributing income from the sale of a service entirely to the state where the service is performed is a questionable practice that fails to recognize the contribution made by the selling activities in the market state to the income of the service enterprise. It can reasonably be contended that market states (see Glossary) are deprived of a fair share of corporate income tax revenues from out-of-state service businesses. Thus the absence of a market-based factor in the apportionment formula increases the benefit for service businesses of locating in states with low taxes or no taxes on corporate income,[9] and may provide multistate businesses with a competitive advantage over wholly in-state service providers.[10]

The "origin-based" sales attribution rule for services also is ill-designed to cope with services whose components are produced in different states. Take, for example, a New York advertising agency that is developing a TV ad campaign for a Chicago company. The campaign draws upon a market research data base programmed and stored on a computer in Massachusetts. The advertising agency has its design office and film studios in Connecticut. As the campaign evolves, presentations sometime are done by teleconference using a rented satellite uplink studio in Connecticut and sometimes in the client's office in Chicago.

The rule provides that the sale should be attributed to the state where the majority of the income-producing activity of the advertising agency occurred, but it would not be easy to make that determination in this example. Tax administrators could legitimately be concerned that the complexity of the transaction would allow the company to attribute the sale to the state with the lowest corporate tax. Conversely, the company would be right to worry that each of the four states would claim the sale, with multiple taxation resulting.

In conclusion, states at least ought to reconsider how to apportion the income of multistate service businesses in response to the increased quantity of services that are being provided across state lines.

Implications for Property Taxation

Many service industries require little tangible property (real estate and equipment) in proportion to their own sales or in proportion to an equal amount of sales by a typical mining or manufacturing company.[11] Often, the value of service companies lies primarily in the expertise of their employees or in intangible assets like a database or a film print. Because of the reduced reliance of many service industries on tangible assets and the abandonment by most states of efforts to tax intangible assets, the shift from production of goods to services is contributing to a relative erosion of the business property tax base. This warrants a reexamination of the role of the property tax in state and local taxation of business.

Conclusion

States have not adequately updated sales taxes, business taxes, and property taxes to reflect the shift toward a service-based economy. This may have produced a competitive disadvantage to producers of goods by allowing some industries and businesses in the service sector to carry a lower direct state and local tax burden.

This situation has important implications for state economic development. States have traditionally emphasized maintaining a competitive manufacturing base because manufactured goods are most likely to be exported from a state. Maintaining a positive balance of trade is critical to economic development. If the goods-producing sector is forced to bear a disproportionate share of the overall state and local tax burden, its profitability and access to capital will be impaired. While the shift away from manufacturing and toward services may represent largely a natural economic evolution, states should be careful not to contribute to the decline of their manufacturing bases by preserving outdated tax systems that shift the burden to manufacturing.

Notes

1. *See* Federation of Tax Administrators, *Sales Taxation of Services—Who Taxes What?* Research Report 137 (Washington, D.C., April 1991) for a discussion of the extent to which states impose the sales tax on service transactions and the issues involved therein. On sales taxes generally, *see* William F. Fox, ed., *Sales Taxation: Critical Issues in Policy and Administration* (Westport, Conn.: Praeger Publishers, 1992).

2. John Mikesell, "State Sales Tax Policy in a Changing Economy: Balancing Political and Economic Logic Against Revenue Needs," *Public Budgeting and Finance* 12, No. 1 (Spring 1992): 88; NCSL calculation based upon Bureau of the Census, State Government Finances, and Survey of Current Business.

3. Based on data presented in John L. Mikesell, "General Sales Tax," in Steven D. Gold, ed. *Reforming State Tax Systems* (Denver, Colo.: National Conference of State Legislatures, December 1986), p. 214 and Mikesell, "State Sales Tax Policy," p. 86. Some of the decline in the yield of the tax is attributable to legislated tax exemptions. In particular, a number of states enacted exemptions for food purchased for home consumption between 1960-1990. Even so, if sales tax productivity had fallen by only one-half its actual drop, the resulting $18 billion

in revenue would have exceeded the total of $15 billion in legislated tax increases in 1991, which was the largest increase in history.

4. Marcia A. Howard, *The Revenue Potential of Taxing Services* (Washington, D.C.: National Association of State Budget Officers, July 1991), pp. 10-15.

5. Howard, *Revenue Potential*; also *see* John L. Mikesell, "Fiscal Effects of Differences in Sales Tax Coverage: Revenue Elasticity, Stability, and Reliance," *1991 Proceedings of the 84th Annual Conference on Taxation of the National Tax Association* (Columbus, Ohio: National Tax Association, 1992), pp. 50-57, and Richard F. Dye and Therese J. McGuire, "Expanding the Sales Tax Base: Implications for Growth and Stability," in Fox, *Sales Taxation*, pp. 169-176; Laird Graeser, "Sales Taxation of Services: An Idea Whose Time Has Come?" in Federation of Tax Administrators, *Sales Taxation of Services*, Research Report 135 (Washington, D.C., October 1990), p. 11.

6. For a comprehensive review of the issues involved in taxing services, *see* William Fox and Matthew Murray, "Economic Aspects of Taxing Services," *National Tax Journal* 41, No. 1, (March 1988): 19-36; Federation of Tax Administrators, *Sales Taxation of Services—Who Taxes What*, and Mindy S. Piatoff, "Difficulties in Structuring A Sales Tax on Services," *State Tax Notes* 3, no. 7 (August 17, 1992): 232-240.

7. Many economists argue that the corporate income tax should be abolished or integrated with the personal income tax so that all income would be taxed only as received by individuals. There is, however, a strong case to be made under the benefits principle of taxation that businesses should be taxed directly for the public services from which they benefit. For example, imagine two equally profitable sole proprietorships operating in a state, one a lawn-cutting company utilizing largely unskilled labor and the other a software development company staffed by computer science graduates of the state university. If the owners of both businesses are taxed equally on their equal personal income, the owner of the lawn cutting business is, arguably, subsidizing the income of the owner of the software company. (Of course, this example also raises the question whether profits are the best measure of the benefits received from the state university, since taxing both businesses on the basis of their equal profits would result in the same degree of cross-subsidization. It could be argued that the "value-added" in the business—which would reflect the higher salaries of the computer programmers—would be a better measure of the relative benefits received by the two companies from state services.)

8. Assuming that the corporation has conducted sufficient activities in the state to cross a threshold subjecting it to the state's corporate tax jurisdiction (a level of activity known as nexus). *See* Glossary.

9. Most investigators who have studied whether differences among state tax burdens on business affect business location decisions have not found significant effects. Other cost factors are more significant; so are state service levels. But most of the research concerns manufacturing, and it may be that service industries are more sensitive to taxes than manufacturers. Such is likely to be the case for businesses like banks, insurance companies, and information services, which have relatively low fixed capital and labor costs and which are principally based on flows of information.

10. Assume, for example, that the provider of an on-line information service has all of its property and 95 percent of its payroll in State A, a state without a corporate income tax. Assume that all of its customers and the other 5 percent of its payroll are in State B, which has a 10 percent corporate income tax. Under the current rules that attribute sales of services on an "origin basis":

$$\frac{100\ \%\ (property) + 95\%\ (payroll) + 100\%\ (sales)}{3} = 98\%$$

of its profits will be apportioned to State A and taxed at a 0 percent rate. The other 2 percent will be taxed by State B at its 10 percent rate.

Under destination-basis rules for the sales factor:

$$\frac{100\%\ (property) + 95\%\ (payroll) + 0\%\ (sales)}{3} = 65\%$$

of the company's profits will be apportioned to State A. The other 35 percent will be apportioned to State B and taxed at its 10 percent rate.

Thus, the destination-basis rules for the attribution of sales reduce the competitive disadvantage that a company with all of its sales, property, and payroll located in State B experiences because of the ability of the first company to locate in State A. Under the destination-basis rules, an additional 33 percent of profits will be taxed at the same 10 percent rate. Of course, because two-thirds of the profits are apportioned on the basis of payroll and sales, the first company still obtains a considerable competitive advantage by locating in State A.

11. Of course, some service industries, like transportation and utilities, have heavy capital requirements.

CHAPTER 7
SHIFTING FROM LOCAL TO INTERNATIONAL BUSINESS

The problem: State tax systems create unintended loopholes and provide competitive advantages to some large interstate and multinational corporations because state tax systems have not been adapted to the increasingly interstate and international character of economic activity.

Everyday experience tells us that relatively few business activities are confined to a single state. The growth of interstate and international commerce involves both transactions and business operations.

A steadily increasing share of transactions are interstate in nature. Millions of homeowners now send their mortgage payments to a bank in another state, for example. The enormous growth in mail-order catalog sales is well-known. More and more businesses operate in more than one state. For example, the local department store may exist in name, but it is likely to belong to a national conglomerate. National franchise operations have replaced mom and pop restaurants.

The extension of economic activity across national boundaries has attracted considerably more attention. As recently as 1970, imports equaled 5.5 percent of gross domestic product, and exports just 5.6 percent. In 1991, the figures were, respectively, 10.9 percent and 10.5 percent.[1] United States corporations owned by foreign corporations accounted for 1.3 percent of total United States corporate assets in 1971. In 1988 that had grown to 7.2 percent.[2]

Like the shift of the economy toward services, the expansion of multistate and multinational business and trade confronts state tax systems with enormous challenges. Because state tax policies have not been appropriately updated, state revenues have suffered and some multistate and multinational businesses enjoy competitive advantages created by tax policy.

Limits on Taxing Multistate and International Business

Definitions of taxing jurisdiction constrain states' ability to tax many multistate businesses and many interstate transactions. Some of these constraints are absolutely necessary; others reflect outdated circumstances. Under the Constitution, a state may not reach outside its borders to tax people, corporations, activities, or transactions unless they have a direct connection to the state or benefit in some manner from services the state provides. Without such a reasonable rule, any state could tax any person or activity anywhere within the United States.

However, these reasonable rules have been unreasonably extended. More than 25 years ago, the United States Supreme Court and Congress erected barriers to the taxation of transactions and income that are properly attributable to states in which businesses' customers are located. The Court did so with respect to state sales and use taxes in its 1967 *National Bellas Hess* decision (the outcome of which was reaffirmed in the *Quill* case decided in May 1992). The Congress did so with respect to state corporate income taxes in enacting Public Law 86-272 in 1959. These barriers are becoming increasingly artificial and costly.

In *Bellas Hess,* the Supreme Court ruled that a state cannot require an out-of-state mail order company to collect the state's use tax from its customers in the state if the company's presence in the state is limited to communicating and transacting business there by United States mail or common carriers (see Glossary). P.L. 86-272 goes further. It prevents a state from imposing a corporate income tax on an out-of-state company selling goods in the state if the company's presence in the state is limited to salespeople soliciting sales that are fulfilled by shipment from out-of-state locations. (This is explained further in the Glossary.)

Since their establishment, the *Bellas Hess* rule and P.L. 86-272 have affected a growing share of transactions and businesses. Untaxed mail-order sales are now estimated to cost state and local governments $3 billion annually.[3] The revenue loss from P.L. 86-272 cannot be measured. However, it has likely grown substantially since the law's enactment, because of the growth in interstate commerce and the increasing sophistication of multistate businesses in taking legal advantage of the law's "safe harbor." The movement away from vertical integration in favor of companies' purchase of intermediate goods from independent suppliers has also probably increased the revenue loss, since traveling sales forces are most likely to be selling to businesses, not to private consumers.

These rules have a further impact. Despite their limited scope, uncertainty about their implications discourages states from updating tax systems to include interstate activities like banking, telecommunications and advertising. Thus the *Bellas Hess* rule and P.L. 86-272 contribute to state revenue losses indirectly as well as directly.

These "physical presence" standards threaten to put a growing share of the potential state tax base out of reach, as developments in computers and telecommunications permit more types of goods and services to be provided across state lines.[4] They also create competitive disadvantages for sellers who are in the same state as their market *vis-à-vis* out-of-state sellers, since the former have to collect sales taxes on transactions when the latter can avoid doing so, and since the former have to pay state corporate income tax on their entire income.

Unintended Tax Advantages for Multistate Businesses

As state and local levies have come to loom larger in their total tax burdens, businesses have understandably devoted greater attention to minimizing their legal tax obligations.[5] The way that a state requires businesses to apportion corporate income for tax purposes between itself and other states is a key issue. More than half of the states with corporate income taxes have retained "separate entity" based apportionment rather than adopting "combined reporting" and have thus provided opportunities for multistate businesses to reduce their total state corporate tax payments by shifting income between states. (See Glossary entry for "combination/combined reporting.")

One increasingly evident form of income shifting involves a corporation's transfer of intangible assets to an affiliated company in a state that offers favorable tax treatment to intangible income, for example, by lacking a corporate income tax or using a low rate. For example, a corporation that plans to sell some stock it owns in another company might first transfer the stock to a subsidiary in a state without an income tax to avoid tax on the capital gains from the sale. In a case now in litigation, a national retailer has transferred its trademark to a "passive investment company" in a state that does not tax such companies and is shifting income from a store in a separate-entity state by having the passive investment company charge the store a royalty for use of the trademark.[6]

States that use separate-entity apportionment frequently have provisions to prevent the use of such techniques when their sole purpose is tax avoidance. But such an intention can be difficult to prove. Separate-entity states do not have a good track record in such cases.[7]

If separate-entity states do not update their laws, they will virtually guarantee the steady erosion of their corporate tax bases. They will also reward interstate companies that can afford good legal advice and shift a growing share of the corporate income tax bill to corporations that cannot afford appropriate legal advice or are too small to have multistate operations. Such tax policy can harm in-state businesses and violates the principle of neutrality by shaping business decisions rather than leaving them to market forces.

Inadequate Coordination of States' Tax Policies

The lack of adequate coordination among state tax policies and administration produces inequitable loopholes that are assuming more and more importance because of the growth of multistate businesses and transactions.

The taxation of television networks offers an example related to corporate income taxes. Some years ago, New York and California, where most networks have their headquarters, changed their rules to allow networks to apportion advertising receipts to all the states that their broadcasts reach in proportion to the size of the audience. Other states ignored the change. Consequently the networks enjoy "nowhere income"—profits that go untaxed by any state.[8] Many other examples of the creation of nowhere income through inadequate coordination of state income tax rules exist.[9]

The lack of interstate coordination in sales taxation is more an issue of policy and administration than it is of laws and regulations. States with sales taxes all have compensating use taxes to eliminate the incentive to buy goods and services in other states with lower rates or exemptions. Use tax, however, is hard to enforce, not only on consumers but also on businesses that are unlikely to be audited regularly for sales tax remittances; examples are retailers who sell only exempt goods or services, and non-retail businesses like wholesalers, construction contractors, and manufacturers.

Convincing Congress to expand the power of states to require out-of-state vendors to collect sales and use taxes would eliminate most use tax evasion.[10] But vendors would still not be required to collect some legally due use taxes because of constitutional limitations or exemptions for small vendors. Thus, states will have to work together more closely to prevent erosion of the sales and use tax base in any case. Some approaches to the problem are discussed in chapter 17.

Inadequate coordination of state taxation of interstate commerce can also lead to double taxation of income or transactions.[11] Indeed, virtually any inconsistency in state rules that has the potential to create "nowhere income" or to allow a transaction to escape tax also has the potential to create multiple taxation. Thus, states certainly need to coordinate their rules to minimize the potential for double taxation. At present, however, double taxation is likely to be a smaller problem than non-taxation. This is due to the combination of stringent limitations on the ability of market states to tax interstate transactions and out-of-state businesses (because of P.L. 86-272 and the *Bellas Hess* rule) and the broad tax exemptions that "origin states" provide for export transactions and export income.

The amount of aggregate base erosion from inadequate coordination of state rules can only be surmised. However, one rough estimate involving corporate taxes found that approximately one-third of total corporate profit reported on federal tax returns was not reported on state tax returns.[12] Since much tax planning is aimed at obtaining a lower rate of taxation rather than complete tax avoidance, this estimate is probably a conservative measure of what states are losing because of their failure to update and coordinate their approaches to interstate taxation.

International Transfer Pricing

Much attention has recently been given to federal revenue losses attributable to multi-national corporations' inappropriate use of transfer-pricing—the practice of using accounting devices to shift profits out of the United States to another jurisdiction that offers tax advantages. International transfer pricing can erode the state corporate income tax base as well (on transfer pricing, see Glossary).

The current concern over transfer pricing originated in statistics showing that foreign-owned corporations in the United States report taxable profits on their U.S. investments substantially lower than those comparable American-owned corporations report.[13] If the return to foreign corporations is really as low as they report, it seems unlikely that the explosion of direct foreign investment in the United States in the 1980s would ever have occurred. One possibility is that profits reported on foreign-owned corporations' tax returns have been reduced by transfer pricing. This possibility has been supported both by econometric research[14] and congressional investigation of the tax returns of foreign-owned companies that have reported little or no taxable income in this country despite having sold billions of dollars worth of consumer goods here.[15]

Evidence indicates that United States-based multinationals also use transfer pricing to shift income abroad.[16] The Internal Revenue Service has pursued a number of major cases against United States-based companies involving the prices set on their sale or licensing of intangibles, such as a patented production process, to their foreign subsidiaries.[17]

Transfer pricing can also be used to shift profits from a corporation located in a high tax state to one located in a low tax state. The states that have adopted combined reporting have long recognized that one of its major benefits is eliminating this potential. However, even the states that require combined reporting by related American companies generally do not require that foreign companies be included.[18] They instead tie their corporate tax base to the federal definition of United States-source income and rely on the Internal Revenue Service to ensure that the transfer prices charged between related United States and foreign corporations are correct. Thus, if the IRS fails at this job, the state corporate tax base suffers.

How well the Internal Revenue Service is preventing federal revenue losses from incorrect transfer prices is a matter of substantial disagreement.[19] The IRS and the Treasury Department have refused to produce any official estimates of the revenue loss.[20] Others' crude estimates are limited to possible tax underpayments by the United States subsidiaries of foreign-owned multinationals. When pressed in a congressional hearing, the IRS commissioner conceded that the data on differential rates of return on assets support an estimated $3 billion annual loss.[21] Some data can be interpreted to support higher estimates of revenue loss. President Clinton cited the figure of $10 billion a year during his campaign.[22]

Foreign-owned multinationals are understandably nervous about becoming the target of discriminatory regulation of transfer pricing. It must be emphasized that there is just as much potential for United States-based companies to engage in aggressive transfer pricing and similar evidence that they are doing so.[23] American corporations and their foreign affiliates do roughly as much business with each other in a year as foreign-owned United States corporations do with their foreign affiliates, offering just as much opportunity to the domestically owned corporations to manipulate transfer prices.[24]

Because reliable figures on the federal revenue loss from transfer pricing are not available, the potential state revenue losses cannot be known. A very rough estimate is possible. Since the weighted-average state corporate income tax rate is between one-quarter and one-fifth of the federal rate, the annual state loss would be between $2 billion and $2.5 billion if the federal loss is $10 billion a year.[25]

In the past few years, Congress has funded more IRS staff to conduct transfer pricing investigations and litigation, involving both United States and foreign-owned companies. It has also expanded the IRS's power to compel companies to reveal their transfer pricing decision making. The IRS and the Treasury Department argue that this is all they need to get the job done.[26] However, a growing number of experts question whether the federal government can act effectively while the IRS carries the burden of proving that the transfer prices of tens of thousands of multinational corporations are incorrect.[27] Other critics have long argued that the arm's length standard not only cannot be administered in a practical sense, but is theoretically flawed as well.[28] Whatever the outcome, the states have a significant stake in it.

Conclusion

The rapid growth in interstate and international commerce confronts the states with significant issues of their authority to tax multi-jurisdictional transactions and businesses, the fair distribution of the tax base among the states, and the preservation of tax bases. Effective solutions to these problems will demand a higher level of interstate coordination and cooperation in tax administration and policymaking than the states have ever attempted before. The states should press the federal government to address the international transfer pricing problem in an effective manner.

Notes

1. U.S. Department of Commerce, *Statistical Abstract of the United States: 1992* (Washington, D.C.: Government Printing Office, 1992), Table 673; "Annual Revisions of the United States National Income and Product Accounts," *Survey of Current Business* 72, no. 7 (July 1992): 11.

2. James R. Hobbs, "Domestic Corporations Controlled by Foreign Persons, 1988," *Statistics of Income Bulletin* 11, no. 2, (Fall 1991): 78.

3. U.S. Advisory Commission on Intergovernmental Relations, *State Taxation of Mail Order Sales: Revised Revenue Estimates, 1990-1992* (December 1991). These estimates are based on the sales of businesses actually classified as direct marketers or mail-order companies. However, use tax is not charged on many interstate sales to businesses by businesses that do not operate primarily as direct marketers. In addition, there is significant evasion of use taxes by people who cross state lines to take advantage of lower rates or exemptions not available in their state of residence. Use tax evasion is a larger problem than the mail-order nexus issue and will remain so until states have greater authority to require vendors to collect the tax.

4. *See*, for example: G. Pascal Zachary, "Industries Find Growth of Digital Electronics Brings in Competitors," *Wall Street Journal*, February 18, 1992; David C. Churbuck and Jeffrey S. Young, "The Virtual Workplace," *Forbes*, November 23, 1992, pp. 184-190; Paul Farhi, "Time Warner Plans 2-Way Cable System," *Washington Post*, January 27, 1993; Gretchen Morgenson, "The Fall of the Mall," *Forbes*, May 24, 1993, pp. 106-112.

5. Companies are making more concerted efforts to minimize their state and local tax payments for at least three reasons. First, the reduction in federal corporate income tax rates in the mid-1980s reduced the value of the deduction for state and local taxes on the federal return. Second, state and local taxes are larger in absolute terms and are thus perceived as a more significant cost factor. Third, many companies have recently faced intensified competition, making them less able to pass on tax costs in the form of higher prices. The competition arises from both the growth in foreign competitors and price deregulation in financial services, telecommunications, etc.

6. *Geoffry, Inc., vs. South Carolina Tax Commission*, Greenville County Circuit Court, February 27, 1992, on appeal to South Carolina Supreme Court.

7. Michael H. Lippman and Rebecca F. Mims-Velarde, "State Challenges to Related Party Structures and Transactions," *State Tax Notes* 2, no. 1 (January 6, 1992): 18-28.

8. Apportionment is discussed in the Glossary. From the example there, it should be evident that unless each of the three apportionment factors totals 100 percent when added for all the states in which a corporation does business, there will be nowhere income. This happens when, for example, New York apportions

a share of its resident TV networks' sales of advertising to Idaho but Idaho continues to treat the sales as all occurring in New York.

9. Many such examples involve very technical details of apportionment rules (e.g., the interaction of "sales throwback" and unitary combination practices involved in the so-called "Finnigan-Joyce" issue in California). Unfortunately, it is on this level of detail that policymakers must focus in order to preserve the corporate income tax as a viable state revenue source.

10. *See* chapter 14 of this report for a discussion of options for reforming the state sales tax.

11. *See*, for example, the recent case of *Exxon Corporation vs. Wyoming Board of Equalization*, 783 P.2d 685 (Wyo. 1989), cert. denied, ___ United States___, 110 S.Ct. 1937 (1990), in which the company was taxed by both Wyoming and Colorado on its purchase of pipe for a pipeline. The United States Supreme Court denied review of the case, leaving Exxon subject to double taxation.

12. Robert P. Strauss, "Considerations on the Federal Collection of State Corporate Income Taxes," *State Tax Notes* 1, no. 3 (September 16, 1991): 82. The estimate takes account of the states that do not impose corporate income taxes. However, it has been criticized for not taking into account various categories of income that are taxable at the federal level but that states cannot or do not choose to tax (e.g., interest on federal obligations, foreign source dividends, "Subpart F" income). The critics have failed to acknowledge that there are countervailing effects from items of income that states tax and the federal government does not (e.g., interest on state and local obligations) and federal deductions that some states do not allow (e.g., dividends received). In any case, the point is not to defend the accuracy of Strauss' estimate to the last dollar, but only to point out that such evidence as exists clearly indicates that it is much more likely that considerable nowhere income exists than that corporations in the aggregate are paying tax on 100 percent of their incomes.

13. Hobbs, "Domestic Corporations Controlled by Foreign Persons, 1988."

14. Harry Grubert, Timothy Goodspeed and Deborah Swenson, "Explaining the Low Taxable Income of Foreign-Controlled Companies in the United States," unpublished paper, November, 1991. This study found that only about half of the difference in reported rates of return on assets between foreign-owned and United States-owned United States corporations could be explained by theoretically supportable explanations *other than* transfer pricing.

15. *See* U.S. Congress, House, Subcommittee on Oversight of the Committee on Ways and Means, *Tax Underpayments by United States Subsidiaries of Foreign Companies, Hearings before the [Subcommittee]*, July 10 and 12, 1990.

16. *See* Lowell Dworin, "Transfer Pricing Issues," *National Tax Journal* 43, no. 3 (September 1990): 285-291.

17. *See* D. Kevin Dolan, "Intercompany Transfer Pricing for the Layman" *Tax Notes* 59, no. 2 (October 8, 1990): 221-227.

18. To be included in a combined report, companies have to be engaged in a unitary business as well as be commonly owned. Although a number of states once included all foreign-incorporated corporations in the combined group, all of them have now eliminated mandatory "worldwide unitary combination." Some states still require combined reporting to include companies that have been

incorporated abroad if more than 20 percent of the company's property and payroll are in the United States

19. Kathleen Matthews, "Just How Much Revenue Could the United States Raise by Beefing-up Transfer Pricing Enforcement?" *Tax Notes International* 5, no. 18 (November 2, 1992): 913-915.

20. Indeed, only one study has been conducted using the IRS data to determine if the problem exists (Grubert, Goodspeed, and Swenson, "Explaining the Low Taxable Income of Foreign Controlled Companies in the United States," and the IRS has not tabulated all of the data it now has available on transactions between foreign-owned United States corporations and their foreign affiliates. *See* James Hobbs and John Latzy, "Transactions Between Foreign Controlled Corporations and Related Foreign Persons," *Statistics of Income Bulletin* 12, no. 1 (Summer 1992): 119-122. The data are tabulated for only the very largest foreign owned United States corporations. Moreover, an enormous body of data collected by the Commerce Department that could shed light on the transfer pricing issue has never been examined for the purpose. These data are contained in the 1987 "benchmark" study of foreign direct investment in the United States and the 1989 benchmark study of direct investment abroad by United States corporations.

21. U.S. Congress, House, Subcommittee on Oversight of the Committee on Ways and Means, *Report on Issues Related to the Compliance with United States Tax Laws by Foreign Firms Operating in the United States*, April 9, 1992, p. 100, for testimony of IRS Commissioner Shirley Peterson.

22. For example, the United States wholesale distributors of foreign manufactured goods devote a considerably higher share of their gross receipts to purchasing the products for resale than do United States wholesalers (a 1988 cost-of-goods sold: sales ratio of 85.6 percent, as opposed to 76.0 percent for United States wholesalers). Hobbs and Latzy, "Transactions Between Foreign Controlled Corporations," p. 83. If the former group experienced the lower ratio of the latter group, they would have had approximately $30 billion more taxable income, and, all other things equal, paid an additional $10 billion in corporate tax. (Multistate Tax Commission staff calculation); Governor Bill Clinton, *Putting People First: A National Economic Stategy for America*, p. 22.

23. Dworin, "Transfer Pricing Issues," and Robert B. Reich, "Does Corporate Nationality Matter?" in U.S. Congress, Joint Economic Committee, *Who is Us? National Interests in an Age of Global Industry*, September 5 and 13, 1990, p. 12.

24. With regard to U.S. subsidiaries of foreign parent multinationals, the IRS Statistics of Income Division has only compiled the data on transactions with related parties for the 121 foreign-controlled U.S. corporations with over $1 billion in sales. The IRS reports a total of $89 billion inbound and outbound transactions for this group of companies, exclusive of the principal amount of loans. *See* James Hobbs and John Latzy, "Transactions Between Foreign-Controlled Corporations and Related Foreign Persons, 1988, Data Release," *Statistics of Income Bulletin*, Summer 1992, p. 122. (This excludes the principal balance of loans from the measure of related party transactions, since only the interest charges on the loans would ordinarily be subject to a Section 482 adjustment.) These 121 corporations, according to IRS, account for approximately half of the total sales of all foreign-controlled corporations. Assuming that the untabulated corporations engage in related-party transactions to the same degree as the tabulated ones, the figures reported for the 121 corporations are doubled,

leading to an estimate of $178 billion of related-party transactions by foreign-owned U.S. corporations.

With regard to U. S. based multinationals, the IRS has compiled data only for the 744 with more than $500 million in assets. *See* John Latzy and Randy Miller, "Controlled Foreign Corporations, 1988," *Statistics of Income Bulletin*, Fall 1992, p. 71. This article (at p. 66) reports $143 billion in related party sales of "stock in trade" with 7,500 foreign subsidiaries. Unpublished data compiled for the Multistate Tax Commission by the Statistics of Income Division counts an additional $33 billion in related party sales of services, royalties, interest, etc. for a total of $176 billion. Since the IRS reports that the 7,500 foreign subsidiaries of the 744 U.S. parents account for fully 92 percent of the sales of all U.S.-controlled foreign subsidiaries, the related party transactions have not been extrapolated upward.

25. Multistate Tax Commission staff estimate.

26. Peterson testimony cited above in note 23.

27. *See* Dale W. Wickham and Charles J. Kerester, "New Directions Needed for Solution of the International Transfer Pricing Puzzle," *Tax Notes* 56, no. 3 (July 20, 1992): 339-361; Louis M. Kauder, "Intercompany Pricing and 482: A Proposal to Shift from Uncontrolled Comparables to Formulary Apportionment Now," *Tax Notes* 58, no. 4 (January 25, 1993): 485-493.

28. *See* Stanley I. Langbein, "Transaction Cost, Production Cost, and Tax Transfer Pricing," *Tax Notes* 44, no. 12 (September 18, 1989): 1391-1413.

CHAPTER 8
FEDERAL PRE-EMPTION OF STATE TAX BASES

The problem: State tax bases are being eroded by federal restrictions more stringent than constitutional limits on state powers to tax.

Changes in the structure of American federalism are eroding state tax bases. While the U.S. Constitution imposes limits on state taxing authority, especially regarding interstate and foreign commerce, the effect of recent federal actions is a degree of pre-emption that far exceeds constitutional provisions.[1] However, states have also failed to seize opportunities to work together to establish joint tax policies and mechanisms that could overcome some of the problems created by federal pre-emption and undercut the rationale for pre-emption.

Statutory and judicial pre-emption. Federal statutes and judicial decisions have restricted state corporate income taxes, have pre-empted certain taxes on real and tangible personal property under the Railroad Revitalization and Regulatory Reform (4R) Act, have limited the states' power to tax airlines in several different ways, and have limited states' ability to collect sales and use taxes from out-of-state vendors (see chapters 6 and 7).[2]

Supreme Court decisions in the 1980s greatly expanded congressional freedom to intrude into matters of state tax policy. Traditional notions of state sovereignty have been withering for many decades, but before the *Garcia* decision in 1985 and South *Carolina vs. Baker* in 1987 the extent of federal power over state and local governments remained uncertain (see Glossary).[3] The Tenth Amendment to the U.S. Constitution was thought to allow states at least the possibility of judicial protection from intrusive federal legislation. In *Garcia*, the court denied the existence of such protections and observed that states had to seek relief in Congress. South *Carolina vs. Baker* applied *Garcia* to a tax case.

The roots of pre-emption. Pre-emption may spring from conflict between states or from a federal intention to seize a revenue base, but more often it is a response to private sector applicants seeking relief from what they consider to be discriminatory taxation by one or more states. Applicants who fail to gain relief from the courts often seek it from Congress. When Congress pre-empts state taxes, it often does so in a manner that generates costly litigation, and the pre-emption severely reduces potential state tax bases.

While states generally abhor federal pre-emption, states also fail to cooperate with each other in ways that could forestall or overcome federal limitations. States could, for example, overcome the limits of the *National Bellas Hess* decision by enacting an interstate compact or uniform law under which participating states would exercise their authority over direct marketers based within their borders to require the collection of the sales and use taxes for the states into which those marketers sell. States could have coordinated a joint litigation defense strategy to resist the excessive judicial expansion of the 4R Act beyond its original intent. They could also have developed uniform, joint procedures for valuing railroad property that might have forestalled negative federal court decisions. In the majority of instances of federal pre-emption, states have alternatives available to them through joint action, but they do not choose to use them.

There is historical precedent for state joint action to block federal pre-emption of state taxing powers. In the late 1960s, when Congress threatened to intervene broadly in state tax affairs through the work of the "Willis Subcommittee," several states developed the Multistate Tax Compact, and that interstate compact successfully forestalled the Willis Committee recommendations. Too often, however, states ignore their potential power to overcome federal pre-emption through joint action.

The 4R Act

The 4R Act is an example of congressional action in response to the entreaties of an aggrieved private interest, and it demonstrates the far-reaching consequences of pre-emptive action taken to benefit a specific industry.

The 4R Act was passed in 1976 after years of complaints from railroads that state property tax practices and policies discriminated against them.[4] Failing to gain relief in the courts, the industry turned to Congress and won privileges unavailable to any other taxpayer. The railroad industry may have had legitimate complaints about state and local taxation. The substance of the complaints is not the issue here. The issue here is whether a federal law is the best way to resolve such issues as opposed to resolving them within or among the states themselves.

The 4R act is a major example of the pitfalls of federal pre-emption because the act, under the guise of "equal" taxation, actually creates inequities:

• It grants railroads direct access to federal courts, bypassing all state courts. Federal courts are not bound by the same tax standards as state courts and do not have as much property tax experience. Thus, railroads can gain advantages in federal court that are not available to other taxpayers.

• It allows railroads to secure injunctions from federal courts that immediately cut off revenue to state and local governments. Injunctions disrupt local budgeting procedures and, as a result, give railroads an unreasonable bargaining advantage in any settlements of 4R tax cases. Again, because of special procedures, railroads secure unfair tax advantages.

• The act ambiguously bans the imposition of *"any other tax,"*[5] which results in discriminatory treatment of a common carrier by railroad. Discrimination is not defined, so railroads are able to challenge in federal court any variation in state and local tax laws they do not like. A number of federal circuit courts have used this provision to give railroads complete exemptions of their personal property on the grounds that exemptions for some types of property that railroads do not even own— e.g. crops and livestock—discriminate against railroads. Because railroads can challenge variations in tax law they dislike, but protect the variations that favor them, they can use the 4R Act to reduce their total tax burden below that of other taxpayers.

The 4R Act began a series of court decisions in Nebraska that disrupted that state's tax system for several years. That kind of disruption is inherent in a federal law that combines broad and ambiguous tax policy language with specific, powerful legal privileges that an industry can use to expand the scope and impact of the law through the federal courts.

Seeing the privileges enjoyed by railroads, other industries want to secure from Congress the same benefits. Congress has already granted some privileges like those in the 4R Act to motor carriers, buses and airlines. Other interstate utilities and carriers seek similar pre-emption of state taxing authority. If any one of them succeeds in winning pre-emption regarding its interests, the pressure to extend similar privileges to other industries is likely to be irresistible.

Mail Order Sales

Judicial limitation of state revenue authority is often based upon interpretation of the interstate commerce clause. One of the best examples is the Supreme Court's pre-emption of states' power to require out-of-state vendors to collect sales tax on many mail order sales (the *Bellas Hess* and *Quill* decisions). The loss of state and local revenue is about $3 billion a year (see chapter 6).[6]

Pre-emption Through Regulatory Authority: The Maryland Gas Guzzler Tax

In addition to statutory and judicial measures, federal regulatory action has recently threatened to become a third avenue toward pre-emption. Possibly the first attempt to pre-empt a state tax through the use of federal regulatory power occurred in 1992 in a statement issued by the National Highway Traffic Safety Administration (NHTSA). The action followed Maryland's imposing a surtax on automobiles with poor fuel economy and a corresponding credit for good fuel economy. NHTSA argues that the state cannot enforce the law because the federal Motor Vehicle and Information and Cost Saving Act pre-empts "any [state] law or regulation *relating* to fuel economy standards."[7] Although the Maryland law does not impose standards, NHTSA officials argue that the federal statutory language should be interpreted broadly to include any tax measure that relates to fuel economy standards.

Beyond the specific issues in this case, however, NHTSA action has broad implications for state tax policy. It could invite further pre-emption of state taxes by federal regulators responding to appeals from individual industries and create a new threat to federalism. The possibility that appointed federal officials could regulate or overrule state tax laws raises a new and extremely serious threat to state sovereignty. Federalism is on trial in the NHTSA action. The issue remains unresolved.[8]

Potential Pre-emptive Threats

A federal value added tax. Many observers feel that a federal value added tax (VAT) is increasingly likely as a means of funding health care or as a means of dealing with the federal deficit. Not only would such a tax raise significant amounts of revenue, some think that it could also have a beneficial effect on saving, investment, and exports, at least when compared with other possible ways of increasing federal taxes.[9]

Creation of a federal European-style VAT would substantially pre-empt state sales tax authority. To allay private sector complaints about the burden of complying with a new national tax in addition to 45 state sales taxes, Congress would face enormous pressure to impose uniform bases and perhaps even rates, and to regulate state administration of sales taxes. An alternative would be the conformity of "piggybacking" of state and federal taxes, including federal collection of the tax with a rebate to the states of their portion.[10]

If the federal VAT takes the form of an operational or "financial statement" type VAT fewer conflicts might occur between federal and state policy, but in all likelihood this version of the VAT would replace the federal corporate income tax. With the base for their own corporate income taxes removed, states would feel compelled to migrate away from corporate income taxes to a state operational VAT piggybacked on the federal operational VAT. The federal government would, by its policy choice, virtually dictate a change in state tax policy.

Commuter taxes and the source tax controversy. Conflict among the states can encourage federal pre-emption. Important recent examples have arisen from state efforts to tax nonresident commuters and retirees.

Disputes regarding commuters have arisen between Maine and New Hampshire and between New York and New Jersey. In each case, the state of employment (Maine and New York, respectively) required all nonresidents employed in the state to count all income including that earned outside the taxing state or by spouses, in determining the appropriate tax rate. Federal court rulings have upheld the practice. Members of Congress from New Hampshire and New Jersey have sought legislation to prohibit states from using this method of calculating income tax rates.

The source tax controversy involves state personal income taxes on retirement income. California, like some other states, taxes pension income earned in the state regardless of the state in which the recipient resides. A California retiree who moves to Nevada or Texas cannot thus escape the California income tax. California and other states support the practice on the grounds that state taxes were deferred while the pension was earned. The courts have upheld the state's position, and retirees have tried to win federal legislation to free them of their obligation.

Conclusion

Federal pre-emption often creates unanticipated problems for the states, and states correctly resist the intrusion of the federal government in state affairs. But when states fail to address issues that cut across state boundaries or to reconcile their competing interests with each other, they can expect federal intervention. Congress will arbitrate between private sector groups and the states or between the states themselves if the states do not resolve the issues in the first instance. States do have a choice: They can significantly increase the degree to which they establish and administer tax policy together and thereby gain greater control over their destiny, or they can ignore the potential power of joint state action and experience increasing federal involvement in what historically have been state matters. The possibilities for state cooperation are discussed further in chapter 17, "Preventing Federal Pre-emption Through Joint State Action."

Notes

1. U.S. Advisory Commission on Intergovernmental Relations, *Federal Statutory Pre-emption of State and Local Authority: History, Inventory and Issues* (Washington, D.C.: 1992).

2. *National Bellas Hess vs. Illinois Department of Revenue*, 386 U.S. 753; *Quill Corporation vs. North Dakota*, 112 S.Ct. 1904 (1992).

3. *Garcia vs. San Antonio Metropolitan Transit Authority*, 469 U.S. 528 (1985); *South Carolina vs. Baker*, 485 U.S. 505 (1988).

4. Objective observers may have concluded that at least some of the railroads' complaints were legitimate. However, the existence of problems in some states does not justify federal intervention affecting all states—especially in the unpredictable way the 4R Act has affected the states. State legislative and judicial processes are the most direct remedy for aggrieved taxpayers, and it is not at all clear that the railroads exhausted those remedies.

5. Emphasis added.

6. Some feel that the Supreme Court's decision making on this issue leaves much to be desired. The Supreme Court allowed 25 years of ambiguity to exist concerning whether or not *Bellas Hess* had been decided on due process or commerce clause grounds—an important matter for determining whether Congress had clear power to address the issue. Moreover, the Court was not equipped to anticipate the long-run consequences of its pre-emption of the states in *Bellas Hess*. The Court never imagined how technological change would facilitate the growth of the direct marketing industry and would reduce the burden of compliance with state and local laws. By 1992, the Court felt it had boxed itself in on the issue. The industry had relied on the earlier decision, and now the Court felt obligated to stick with the old ruling, even while stating that it might have decided the issue differently if it were confronting it for the first time in *Quill*. The judicial process in this case has proven short-sighted and inflexible. Having not anticipated in 1967 the long-term changes that would occur, the Court in 1992 was unwilling to recognize the implications of those changes when confronted again with the mail order issue. Thus, courts should be more careful in pre-empting state taxing powers, because decisions that limit state powers (as opposed to those expanding state powers) have proven to be inflexible even in the face of changes that undermine the rationale for the decisions.

7. Emphasis added.

8. The issue remained unresolved in May 1993.

9. *See* for example, U.S. Department of Treasury, Office of Tax Policy, *Restructuring the U.S. Tax System for the 21st Century: An Option for Fundamental Reform* (Washington, D.C., December 10, 1992), calling for a business transfer tax.

10. *See* Charles E. McClure Jr., "State and Local Implication of a Federal Value Added Tax," in Federation of Tax Administrators, *Revenue Administration—1989, Proceedings of the 57th Annual Meeting* (Washington, D.C., 1990), pp 150-158; Alice M. Rivlin, *Reviving the American Dream: The Economy, the States, and the Federal Government* (Washington, D.C.: The Brookings Institution, 1992), pp. 142-152.

CHAPTER 9
DECLINE OF THE ROLE OF THE PROPERTY TAX

The problem: State and local governments continue to shift revenue reliance away from the property tax, placing a heavier burden on other revenue sources.

Voters' dislike of the property tax has driven many state and local decisions on taxes and spending over the past 20 years. Since the early 1900s, state-local finance has been characterized by a shift in reliance from property taxes to income and sales taxes, and there is every reason to assume that voters want this tax shift to continue. This is not so much the "rebellion" against the property tax so beloved of headline writers as it is an evolutionary change in American public finance. The challenge for state and local governments comes in finding substitute revenues or spending reductions.

The shift away from property taxes has reduced the regressivity of state tax systems and helped reduce fiscal disparities between rich and poor local governments. However, shifting the revenue burden to sales and income taxes has exacerbated revenue fluctuations caused by economic cycles and placed new strains on state revenue systems.

This chapter examines the change in state and local reliance upon property taxes over the last 20 years, the role of the property tax revolt in accelerating the decline in reliance on property taxes, and the implications of this tax shift for the future of state revenue systems.

Changes in Reliance on Property Taxes

The movement away from property taxes. Figure 9 illustrates the declining role of the property tax in state-local finance. The property tax share of state and local tax collections fell from 39.2 percent in 1970 to 29.9 percent in 1986, before rebounding slightly to 31 percent in 1990. Throughout this period, reliance on state and local sales taxes has grown a little, and reliance on personal income taxes has grown sharply (see chapter 2 of this report). This represents the substitution of taxes enacted and collected by state government for taxes levied by local governments. It also reflects local governments' shift from property taxes to user charges and fees.

This tax shift is also reflected in a decline in property tax collections as a percentage of personal income. Property tax collections dropped from about 4 percent of personal income in 1978 to 3.3 percent in 1984, rebounding to 3.4 percent in 1990. Most states fit this general pattern, although there are some notable exceptions. More dramatic reductions occurred in California and Massachusetts, where property tax limitations were approved in 1978 and 1980, respectively.

The tax revolt. The property tax revolt that swept the initiative states in the late-1970s accelerated the shift in reliance away from property taxes. A brief summary of the response to passage of tax revolt measures in California and Massachusetts illustrates the impact of these measures on the respective state revenue systems.

Figure 9
Property Taxes as a Percentage of State and Local Tax Collections, 1970-1990

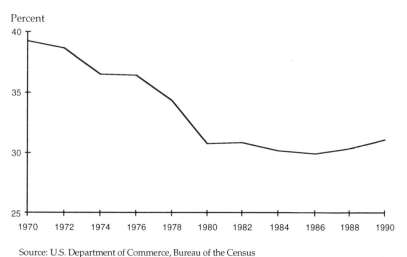

Source: U.S. Department of Commerce, Bureau of the Census

Proposition 13 reduced local government revenue in California by $7 billion in just one fiscal year, forcing the state (which had a surplus) to assume funding for over $1.5 billion in county programs. The state share of total state and local tax revenue jumped from 55 percent to 66 percent as state spending and taxes were substituted for local property taxes.

In Massachusetts, the state enacted a major revenue sharing program in response to voter approval of Proposition 2 1/2 in 1980. This initiative capped local property tax revenue increases to 2.5 percent annually and limited total property tax levies to 2.5 percent of a property's market value. The state's share of total state and local revenue increased from 57 percent to 66 percent between 1978 and 1990.

Beyond its direct impact on the state-local revenue systems in the tax revolt states, the property tax revolt also led other states to re-examine the role of the property tax in their revenue systems. States assumed a more important role in financing government services and state-local tax systems became less regressive as state income taxes were substituted for property taxes.

However, the growing use of income and consumption taxes made revenue systems more susceptible to economic cycles. California and Massachusetts were among the states forced to cut state aid to local governments most sharply during the 1991-92 economic downturn.

The tax revolt outlook. The outlook for future property tax limitations is mixed. Fewer than half of the states have the initiative process, and most of those are Western states where limitations have already passed or where property taxes are well below the national average. In 1992, voters rejected sweeping property tax rollbacks in Michigan and Idaho but approved limitations on the growth of property taxes in Colorado and Florida.

Despite their limited success in recent elections, property tax limitations remain a very real threat to state revenue systems. For example, Oregon voters approved a property tax rate rollback in 1990 that requires the state to reimburse school districts for all the revenues they lost due to the rollback. When the limitation is fully phased in, the state will be forced to increase its spending on schools by almost $1.5 billion annually. In Michigan in 1993 the legislature repealed the authorization for school districts to levy property taxes for operations.

The Implications of Reduced Reliance on Property Taxes

As mentioned above, states have substituted state taxes and spending for local spending financed through property taxes. However, local governments have also increased their reliance on local sales and income taxes, user fees, and charges.

Between 1970 and 1990, the property tax share of all local tax collections declined in 41 states, while in 21 of these states non-property tax reliance increased by more than 10 percentage points. Nationally, local reliance on taxes other than the property tax jumped from 15.1 percent to 25.6 percent.

Local option taxes. Local option taxes have the benefit of allowing local governments to reduce property taxes. However, local option taxes also reduce state control over these tax sources and limit a state's ability to raise additional revenue by increasing tax rates.

This is particularly true with the sales tax, which is the most common local option tax. As indicated in table 6, taxpayers in portions of eight states pay combined state and local sales tax rates of eight percent or more, while taxpayers in two states—Alabama and Louisiana—pay nine percent or more. These high rates are particularly hard on the poor and create problems of tax avoidance and other distortions of economic behavior. Some states find that their options for increasing sales tax rates are limited by high combined rates.

Table 6
Combined State-Local General Sales Tax Rates in Selected Cities, 1992

State	City	Local Rate	Combined State and Local Rate
Rate 9 percent or more:			
Alabama	Mobile	4.5%	9.5%
Louisiana	New Orleans	5.0	9.0
	Baton Rouge	6.0	10.0
Rate 8 percent or more:			
California	Los Angeles	2.25	8.25
	San Francisco	2.25	8.25
	San Diego	2.25	8.25
Illinois	Chicago	2.50	8.75
New York	New York	4.25	8.25
	Buffalo	4.0	8.0
	Yonkers	4.25	8.25
Tennessee	Memphis	2.25	8.25
	Nashville	2.25	8.25
Texas	Austin	1.75	8.0
	Dallas	2.0	8.25
	Houston	2.0	8.25
Washington	Seattle	1.7	8.2

Source: U.S. Advisory Commission on Intergovernmental Relations, *Significant Features of Fiscal Federalism*, Volume 1: 1992, pp. 98-101. Updated by NCSL survey data.

This problem appears to be less pronounced with local option income taxes, which are much less prevalent than local sales taxes. Local governments in 11 states collected income taxes in 1990, but in only four of these states were collections above 20 percent of all local tax collections. School districts in Ohio and Pennsylvania collect income taxes, but rates are generally low (except in Philadelphia). Kentucky counties receive about one-quarter of their tax revenue from income taxes, but combined state and local rates are low by national standards.

Maryland may be the only state where combined state and local income taxes are high enough to limit state options. Maryland increased the allowable local option income tax from 50 percent of state tax liability to 60 percent in 1992.

User fees and charges. The share of state and local own source general revenues derived from user fees, charges, and other miscellaneous revenues has grown steadily and significantly over the past 20 years. As shown in Table 7, the share of local revenues from charges, interest, and miscellaneous revenue has grown from 24.4 percent in 1970 to 37.5 percent in 1990.

Table 7
Percentage Distribution of Selected Categories of State and Local Own-Source Revenue, 1970 and 1990

	State		Local	
	1970	1990	1970	1990
Tax Revenue	83.4%	76.8%	75.6%	62.5%
Charges and				
Miscellaneous	14.1	16.2	21.4	27.7
Net Interest	2.5	7.0	3.0	9.8
Total	100.0%	100.0%	100.0%	100.0%

Federal aid is excluded from the totals.

Source: U.S. Department of Commerce, Bureau of the Census, *Government Finances*

Charges and miscellaneous general revenues grew from 21.4 percent to 27.7 percent of local own-source revenues over the period. Also noteworthy is the growth in local interest revenues, up from 3 percent to 9.8 percent of local own-source revenues. This increase may be attributable to improved cash management practices and the increased use of trust funds by local governments.

Conclusion

The local shift to non-tax sources, the growth in local option tax alternatives, and the shift in program funding responsibility to the states have helped reduce the burden of the property tax. Property tax revenues have fallen from 4.3 percent of personal income in 1970 to 3.4 percent in 1990. While property tax levels have rebounded from their mid-1980s lows, they are unlikely to approach the levels of the 1970s.

Reduced reliance on the property tax is a double-edged sword for state-local finance. Shifting reliance from property to income taxes has made tax systems less regressive. The shift has addressed taxpayer concerns about the fairness of the property tax. Also, broadening the base from local to statewide tax sources has helped reduce fiscal disparities in education funding.

On the flip side, however, the property tax is one of the most stable state or local tax sources in times of recession. The shift away from property taxes has exacerbated the fiscal problems of state and local governments in the 1990s. And to the extent that local governments share state tax bases through local option sales and income taxes, states find their revenue-raising options narrowed.

Fiscal centralization has left states with more responsibility to fund programs from their revenue bases. Many of these added responsibilities, added when state fiscal conditions were strong, have placed severe strains upon state revenue systems in the 1990s.

CHAPTER 10
PERSONAL INCOME TAXES

The problem: Changes in the U.S. economy and demographic patterns pose growing problems for the base and equity of the state personal income tax as well as its responsiveness to personal income growth.

axes on individual incomes have become an increasingly important component of state tax systems over the past 40 years; they now produce almost as much revenue as the general sales tax. Forty-one states and the District of Columbia levy a broad-based personal income tax.[1] While the personal income tax is in many ways a success story in state taxation,[2] a number of problems affect it. Many of the problems parallel those of the federal income tax, but others are peculiar to the state tax.

Growth of Fringe Benefits
Over time, an increasing proportion of American worker compensation has been paid in the form of fringe benefits and other non-monetary compensation not subject to the federal income tax, such as pre-tax contributions to pension plans, health insurance, various forms of deferred compensation, and flexible spending accounts.[3] Since state income tax bases generally conform to the federal tax base, this income largely goes untaxed at the state level as well.[4] Without a change in tax policy or patterns of compensating workers, the relative elasticity of the personal income tax will continue to decline steadily. Moreover, workers can receive similar total compensation but substantially different untaxed benefits, which will produce disparities in the treatment of similarly situated taxpayers as long as fringe benefits are tax-exempt.[5]

Other Exemptions and Exclusions
In addition to the base erosion arising from conformity to the federal tax code, states have independently enacted exemptions, deductions, and exclusions which further erode the tax base, raise issues of horizontal equity, and reduce elasticity. In particular, nine states allow a total or partial deduction for federal taxes paid which drastically reduces the effective state tax base and favors upper income taxpayers more than lower income taxpayers.[6] Other relatively common preferences include exempting interest on state and local debt obligations (sometimes including those of other states), credits for other state and local taxes, and (for sole proprietorships, partnerships, and S-corporations) economic development-related credits and allowances.

The Aging Population

In addition, many states have enacted some form of tax preference for certain types of income earned by the elderly: targeted tax credits and enhanced deductions, exemptions, and exclusions.[7] Policymakers need to recognize that the relative cost of these preferences will rise disproportionately as the U.S. population grows older and greater proportions of income and/or taxpayers are eligible for the preference (see chapter 4).[8]

Forms of Business Organization

As discussed in chapter 7, businesses are increasingly organizing in partnerships, subchapter S corporations, and other non-traditional forms. In principle, such steps should not affect personal income taxation since the income flowing through such entities should be reported on individual returns. As a practical matter, the administrative complexity of tracking such income and taxpayers is considerable for most states, especially with regard to nonresident taxpayers. There are also compliance burdens for taxpayers in filing returns with multiple states when such entities conduct commerce across state lines.

Federal Conformity

While federal linkage is a widespread and generally positive feature of state income tax systems, it does create some complications. Nearly every federal change alters the state tax, and this can cause problems of stability and reliability in state revenues. Given the propensity of the federal government to tinker with the tax code, state tax policymakers find themselves revisiting their tax laws more frequently than would be desirable, at times after they have finalized their budget plans for the year. Conformity also places states in the somewhat incongruous position at times of subsidizing their residents for activities undertaken in other states, like interest costs associated with a vacation or rental home in another state.

Increased Mobility

The increased mobility of U.S. taxpayers leads to two problems for state income taxes. The first involves the taxation of interstate commuters and others who regularly work in one or more states in which they do not reside.[9] People who regularly work in a number of different states are liable for tax in each state. This imposes a significant compliance burden on the individual who must file multiple tax returns; it also imposes burdens on the state tax agency to enforce compliance with the filing requirements on an efficient and equitable basis.

The second problem involves the appropriate and effective taxation of deferred income (i.e., retirement and pension income) when recipient taxpayers retire in a state other than the one in which the income originated.[10] Having received a tax deferment while earning income in the state, the individual now receives the retirement benefit in another state (perhaps with no income tax). Some states (notably California) require out-of-state recipients of deferred income to pay tax on retirement income earned from services previously performed in the state. Collection of the tax by the "source" state presents practical difficulties that can lead to uneven enforcement. Retirees of course face a compliance burden, particularly if they have worked in several states. These difficulties and burdens (as well as a belief by some that the "source" state should not tax such income) has led to calls for federal legislation to limit states' ability to tax nonresident pension income. (See chapter 8 on the issue of pre-emption.)

Encroachments on Deductibility

As Congress anxiously casts about for new revenue, federal tax writers increasingly view the deductibility of state tax income taxes with a jealous eye. Deductibility of state sales taxes was a casualty of the 1986 Tax Reform Act. The growing federal tendency to regard state government as just another special interest group endangers the deductibility of state personal income taxes. The Omnibus Budget Reconciliation Act of 1990 imposed the first limit on such deductibility since the institution of the federal income tax.[11] Any limitation on deductibility increases the effective burden of the state tax.

Rate Structure

The 1986 Tax Reform Act reduced the graduation in marginal federal tax rates. In many cases, states followed suit and reduced the progressivity of their rate structure.[12] Coupled with an increasing concentration of income at the upper end of the income scale, the result is a loss of elasticity in the personal income tax. There may also be a decline in the progressivity of the tax as a whole.13

Conclusion

The state personal income tax is not only a source of state revenue rivaling sales and use taxes, but is also a source of balance against the regressive character of most other state taxes. Despite its importance, a number of factors are eating away at the breadth of the income tax base and the progressivity of the tax. Because of the linkage between the federal personal income tax and that of most states, states' freedom to maneuver is already limited. Ways to address the problems discussed here appear in chapter 13 of this report.

Notes

1. Tennessee and New Hampshire also levy a personal income tax on certain interest and dividend income only.

2. Increased reliance on the income tax has reduced the regressivity of the tax structure and has reduced reliance on the ad valorem property tax by providing a revenue source for local aid in many states.

3. In 1960, employer contributions to social insurance and pension, health, and welfare funds amounted to 8 percent of total employee compensation. In 1991, these benefits amounted to $580 billion or 17 percent of total compensation. Source: Council of Economic Advisors, *Economic Report of the President* (Washington, DC: U.S. Government Printing Office, February 1992), p. 322.

4. All but five states conform their income tax bases to the federal tax base by specifying in law a federal "starting point" (adjusted gross income, taxable income, or tax liability) for the computation of state tax. The effect is for the state tax to incorporate all federal tax code features up to the specified starting point unless state law otherwise so provides. In some states, annual or periodic legislation is required to update the conformity to the federal code. For further discussion, see Federation of Tax Administrators, *Impact of Federal Tax Changes on State Income Taxes* (Washington, D.C., February 1992).

5. The estimated federal revenue effect for the exclusion of employer contributions to pension plans is $51 billion in 1992 and for employer-paid medical insurance premiums it is $42 billion. These are the two largest individual federal tax expenditures. Source: Office of Management and Budget, *Budget Baselines, Historical Data, and Alternatives for the Future* (Washington, D.C.: U.S. Government Printing Office, 1993), pp. 546-562.

6. *See* Federation of Tax Administrators, *Impact of Federal Tax Changes on State Income Taxes*, p. 5. Note that since publication of the paper, Kansas has repealed its optional tables allowing a deduction for federal taxes paid.

7. For an excellent review of the nature of preferences for the elderly and senior citizens, *see* Keith Carlson, "State Income Tax Treatment of Senior Citizens Changing," *State Tax Notes* 2, no. 6 (February 10, 1992): 192-200.

8. In 1960, 9.2 percent of the U.S. population was over age 65; by 1990 this had risen to 12.5 percent. The proportion of the population over age 65 will remain relatively stable through the year 2010. Over the ensuing 20 years, the number of elderly will increase by 93 percent as the Baby Boom reaches age 65. By 2030, over one in five U.S. residents will be over age 65. Source: Cynthia Taeuber, *Sixty-five Plus in America*, Current Population Reports, Special Studies, P. 23-178 (Washington, D.C.: U.S. Department of Commerce, Bureau of the Census, August 1992).

9. Most states impose their tax on a "source" basis, meaning that income is taxed in the state where the services giving rise to the compensation were performed or where it is earned, rather than necessarily being taxed in the state in which the worker resides. This method was upheld by the U.S. Supreme Court a number of years ago in *Shaffer vs. Carter*, 252 U.S. 37 (1920). Certain states (e.g., Virginia, Maryland, and D.C.) have entered agreements to tax workers on a reciprocal basis in their state of residency.

10. For a complete discussion, see Walter Hellerstein and James Charles Smith, "State Taxation of Nonresidents' Pension Income," *State Tax Notes* 2, no. 27 (July 6, 1992): 16-24.

11. The Act placed a limit on certain itemized deductions for households with over $100,000 in AGI. Certain itemized deductions will be reduced by an amount equal to 3 percent of the income over $100,000. Medical expenses, investment interest, and theft and casualty losses are excluded from the disallowance, and the disallowance may not reduce total itemized deductions by more than 20 percent.

12. At least 16 states reduced marginal tax rates in the two years following the federal Tax Reform Act. Several states have always had a flat-rate income tax, e.g., Massachusetts, Pennsylvania, Illinois, Indiana, and Michigan. *See* Steven D. Gold, "A Review of Recent State Tax Reform Activity," in Steven D. Gold, ed., *The Unfinished Agenda for State Tax Reform*, pp. 17-23.

13. The degree of graduation in the rate structure is only one determinant of whether the tax has a progressive distribution. Other features such as personal exemptions or credits, standard and itemized deductions, tax credits, and the breadth of the tax base will determine the final distribution of the tax burden across income groups.

SECTION 3
OPTIONS FOR CHANGE

This section summarizes possible responses to the problems with state tax systems, and has two major themes. One major theme is that of broadening state tax bases, in response to the point made throughout section 2 that state tax bases have not been adapted to economic and demographic changes, and that federal pre-emption and to some extent interstate tax competition have made the situation worse. The section evaluates possible ways to expand the base of the corporate income tax in response to changes in business methods and organization, and weighs the pros and cons of expanding state sales tax bases to more services. It discusses the value added tax as one possible solution to many of the problems state tax systems now experience.

The second major theme of section 3 is the need for greater cooperation among the states in the analysis, design, enactment, and administration of tax policy. State tax systems now operate in a national or even a global economy. The competitiveness that has traditionally characterized state tax policy is increasingly expensive to both the private and the public sectors. Competing, overlapping, and piecemeal tax systems—the result of uncoordinated state enactments—increase compliance costs, pose the risk of double taxation, create tax inequities, and can have adverse consequences for economic growth as well as limiting state tax systems' ability to respond to national economic growth. This theme is explicit in chapters 11 and 17, and it is implicit throughout the section.

CHAPTER 11
INTERSTATE TAX COMPETITION

Interstate tax competition occurs in many forms and varieties. Some can be beneficial in promoting broad tax bases and efficient government. Others reduce state tax bases and deter modernization of state tax systems. There is no apparent consensus on the relationship between state tax competition and economic development.

Developing concrete suggestions to reduce interstate competition is difficult. Although a rigorous analysis of many tax incentives would probably conclude that their stimulative effect is minimal, it is unlikely that states will engage in wholesale repeal of such measures. In fact, states are more likely to enact new incentives.[1] This being the case, states should focus their efforts on improving the information available to policymakers and promoting uniformity among states in order to reduce the undesirable effects of interstate tax competition.

Too often, state debates over enactment of a tax incentive or exemption center on the need to match some particular incentive offered by another state instead of the total tax structure of the two states. Accurate evaluation of the need for an incentive should begin with an understanding of a state's overall tax burden on business and the relationship between taxes and business finances. Viewing the larger picture can help policymakers avoid unnecessary or improperly structured tax incentives, while giving them a better understanding of the impact of the overall tax structure.

If state policymakers wish to use the tax code to encourage a specific kind of behavior, they should target the incentive as closely as possible to their strategic objective. Tax incentives cannot be the entirety of a development strategy. They are just one part of a broader strategy which should be designed to display the strengths of the state concession.[2] Revenue losses can be minimized by targeting the incentive to particular types of industries. While this approach violates the principle of horizontal equity, it minimizes the impact on the tax base while making the concession more manageable.

It is a mistake to leave tax incentives in place without systematic and regular evaluations of their impact. This of course requires a clear idea of the impact the incentives were supposed to have—improvement in state revenue collections, creation of jobs, or some other measurable goal. It is helpful to impose a sunset date on each incentive and to require that a thorough evaluation be undertaken before it is renewed. At the very least, some analysis will be done and belief in the incentive will be reaffirmed. Some states have developed criteria for analyzing requests for financial incentives that could help with such a review.[3]

In analyzing the potential benefits from granting a special incentive, state officials have to make assumptions about the impact of the new business development. Variations in these assumptions could cause one state to view the project more positively than another, and to inflate its incentives (and the bidding) unrealistically. States might be able to improve the information they use for formulating proposals by working together to arrive at some common assumptions or estimates about the impact of the development in terms of the number of primary jobs, secondary jobs, service needs, and the like. Common knowledge of the project might help limit the scope of a bidding war and prevent and reduce the ability of the object of the bids to play one party off against another.

Incentives sometimes breed public distrust of government. To prevent this, states might consider "showing the people what they are buying" by requiring that recipients disclose the value of the incentives they receive and the performance requirements on which the incentives were based—creation of new jobs or whatever—and the actions the recipient undertook in response. Such a practice would increase the need to set measurable expectations for recipients of concessions as well as put pressure on both the recipients and grantors of benefits to account for the value of the concessions.

As discussed elsewhere in this report, interstate competition impedes the modernization of state tax systems, and greater cooperation and uniformity in tax policymaking are necessary. This has led Alice Rivlin, deputy director of the Office of Management and Budget, to suggest that states need to adopt one or more common taxes—the bases of which would be defined uniformly for all the states—in order to eliminate interstate competition with respect to at least that dimension. The shared tax approach could be used with a corporation income tax, value added tax, sales tax, or fuel tax and could be implemented through either state or federal government action. While a number of variations on the theme are possible, the noteworthy point in Rivlin's analysis is that cooperative state policymaking and consistent tax policies are essential steps toward eliminating competition and ensuring the long-term vitality of state tax systems.[4]

Conclusion

Interstate tax competition and the use of tax incentives are and will continue to be part of the state tax policy landscape. To the extent that competition can promote efficiency in government and tax systems it can be beneficial. The greater likelihood is that competition and incentives will erode state tax bases. Some modest procedural reforms might help to mitigate these undesirable consequences. Overcoming the chilling effect of competition on state efforts to upgrade their revenue systems, however, will require a new level of cooperative action among the states.

Notes

1. A recent Council of State Governments report found that 70 percent of the states considered that the packaging of financial and tax incentives to stimulate business development is an "important" issue, and 64 percent of the states felt pressure to offer "better" incentives than other states. Lee Walker, *The Changing Arena: State Strategic Economic Development* (Lexington, Kentucky: Council of State Governments, 1989), p. 12-14.

2. Mark Muchow pointed out how other, more direct means would be better at job creation than the super credit on new investment. *See* Mark Muchow, "The West Virginia Investment Tax Credit Experience." Jane Gravelle came to similar conclusions in examining enterprise zone incentives in "Enterprise Zones: The Design of Tax Subsidies," Congressional Research Service Paper, Washington, D.C., June 3, 1992.

3. Beyond specific incentives, the Council of State Governments has developed recommendations encouraging states to rethink their entire approach to promoting economic development by developing strategic approaches to development, concentrating on a "stable and equitable" fiscal system and improved information and analysis. *See* Lee Walker, *The Changing Arena: State Strategic Economic Development*, pp. 26-27. This report also discusses the guidelines some states (notably Wisconsin) have developed to evaluate the requests for financial incentives.

4. *See* Alice M. Rivlin, *Reviving the American Dream: The Economy, the States, & the Federal Government* (Washington, D.C.: The Brookings Institution, 1992), pp. 142-52. Rivlin arrives at a recommendation for a common, shared tax to upgrade state revenue systems as part of redefining the roles and responsibilities of the federal and state governments.

CHAPTER 12
RETAIL SALES AND USE TAXES

The state general sales tax is the most important source of state tax revenue, but its role is threatened by its very structure, as discussed at various places in section 2 of this report.[1] Its main shortcoming is its inelasticity—its failure to grow proportionately in response to growth in the economy. The inelasticity occurs because of the exclusion of services from the base, legislatively enacted exemptions, and the inability of states to collect use taxes on many interstate transactions. There are other problems with the sales tax. It is regressive in its incidence across income groups. Although it is intended to tax final personal consumption, many business transactions are taxed, which leads to pyramiding.

Expanding the Sales Tax to Service Transactions

The most common prescription for many of these ailments is to broaden the base to include service transactions, already the practice in Hawaii, New Mexico, and South Dakota, and recently considered in many other states.[2] Putting this prescription into effect involves difficult policy and administrative issues. They include tax pyramiding if business services are included, taxing interstate service transactions, interstate competitiveness, and the regressivity of the tax.[3]

Pyramiding and the taxation of business services. If a state extends its sales tax to services consumed by businesses, like data processing or advertising, it will face the issue of tax pyramiding. Tax pyramiding occurs when the sales tax is imposed on goods or services used in the production of other goods, rather than being imposed only on final consumption. A portion of this intermediate tax will be passed on to the purchaser of the product, and a certain amount of double taxation will occur. Pyramiding causes the actual distribution of the tax burden to vary with the nature of the industry. Taxing business services can also be a disadvantage to small businesses that cannot hire staff to perform the taxed services internally and so avoid the tax as larger firms can.

Pyramiding occurs already because of sales taxes on business purchases of tangible goods, but provisions exist to minimize it, such as exemptions of capital equipment, packaging, goods for resale, and goods incorporated in manufactured products.[4] Such provisions are more difficult to apply to services. As a result, some analysts have suggested that the taxation of business services (as opposed to consumer services) should be avoided altogether.[5] Others have avoided this "all or nothing" view and argued that expanded concepts of "sale for resale" and "processing" exemptions could also be made to apply in the services area.[6]

At times the argument for excluding business inputs from the sales tax is taken to the point of suggesting that all business purchases of tangible property be excluded from the tax.[7] This would have serious revenue effects in most states and could invite tax evasion. However, the elimination of pyramiding could be achieved through a program of business tax reform that included adoption of a broad-based value added tax as a substitute for a variety of current business levies. (See the discussion in chapter 15.)

Interstate transactions. Perhaps the most intractable issue faced by states that have considered sales taxation of services has been administration of the use tax on interstate service transactions. In imposing the sales tax on services, states seek to create a level playing field where an in-state provider may sell services out-of-state without collection of the tax and where the tax is imposed on services purchased from an out-of-state supplier. Otherwise, in-state vendors will be at a disadvantage in competing for business outside the state and in competing with out-of-state providers.

For tangible personal property, states impose a compensating use tax to equalize the tax burden on goods purchased in-state and out-of-state. A use tax on the purchase of taxable services is somewhat more difficult to administer since there is nothing tangible to which to attach the tax, thus making it harder to decide where the service is "used, consumed, or enjoyed." Some services may be performed or used in several states, which makes determining the appropriate state for taxation or the appropriate portion of the transaction to tax a difficult matter. This is particularly true of general business services like accounting, consulting, and legal counsel provided to enterprises doing business in several states. State legal jurisdiction to tax (called *nexus*) remains an area of uncertainty with many household services that can be provided through telecommunications, such as direct broadcast television and on-line computer services.

States have taken two approaches to these issues. Hawaii and New Mexico have provided that services performed in the state and used outside the state are exempt from tax. With some exceptions, however, neither state attempts to impose a use tax on services purchased outside the state for in-state use largely because of the relatively closed nature of the economy of these two states.

Florida and Massachusetts (in their laws that were subsequently repealed) designed a use tax on "in-bound" service transactions.[8] For transactions where the "use" could not be pinpointed, these two states apportioned the value of the services to themselves for tax purposes according to the standard three-factor formula (property, payroll, and sales) used for state income tax purposes. They effectively said that these categories of service are taxable in the state to the extent that the buyer carries on business in the state.[9]

Interstate competitiveness. The effect of taxing services on the cost of doing business in a state is also an issue to be addressed. This is commonly characterized as, "Can a state afford to be different from its neighbors?" Traditional sales taxes, levied on the consumer, should not affect business competitiveness. But the inclusion of business services within the tax can raise the cost of doing business in one state over another and thus have an impact on a state's competitiveness.[10]

Regressivity. Whether the extension of the sales tax to services increases or reduces regressivity will depend on the services taxed and the current base of the tax. However, it is an error to address regressivity in the context of only the sales tax or any other single tax. The issue has to be seen in the context of the entire state and local revenue burden. For example, income tax credits or direct refund payments can be targeted to the desired population. Hawaii currently taxes services in a comprehensive manner and uses various rebate and credit mechanisms to mitigate regressivity, and in other states income tax credits for low-income people address sales tax regressivity.

Summary: expansion of sales taxes to services. In assessing an expansion of the sales tax to services, states should be careful "not to lose sight of the forest for the trees." Any serious difficulty in sourcing interstate transactions is limited to a small number of services not involving real property or tangible personal property. Moreover, in many states there are significant opportunities for expanding the sales tax base before reaching business services. Particular areas worthy of examination include personal services (e.g., hair care and health clubs), utility services, admissions and amusements, and repair and installation services. Taxation of these services can generally be implemented with relatively few administrative problems.[11]

Broadening the Base to Exempt Goods

States have narrowed the sales tax base through exempting many goods, particularly household necessities and groceries, as a means of reducing the impact of the sales tax on low-income households.[12] Such exemptions reduce the tax base, diminish the rate of revenue growth, and increase the volatility of the tax.[13] Exempting food for home consumption has a significant effect on sales tax collections and rates. In a 1992 survey, 22 states that exempt food for home consumption estimated the foregone revenues to average 16.5 percent of existing sales tax collections. Such states have, on average, a sales tax rate one percentage point higher than states whose sales tax base includes food for home consumption.[14]

Such exemptions are intended to benefit low-income households. The need for them has been somewhat reduced by the federal provision prohibiting collection of sales taxes on food purchased with food stamps (which are now used by more than 10 percent of all American families). Moreover, they are an expensive way to reduce the tax burden on the poor because they are not targeted to that group and tend to provide benefits of greater monetary value to upper income households.[15] Exemptions for food, nonprescription drugs and health aids also raise serious administrative and compliance issues.[16]

Seven states—Hawaii, Idaho, Kansas, New Mexico, South Dakota, Vermont, and Wyoming—currently use tax credits, rather than exemptions, to provide sales tax relief to the intended populations instead of exempting some or all of these items.[17] These programs, operating through the income tax or as stand-alone payment programs, provide refundable tax credits to poorer households to compensate them for paying sales taxes on food or other necessities. The tax credit approach improves the stability of the tax system, better targets the tax relief, and reduces substantially the revenue impact of the relief.

On the other hand, it is true that tax credits may be less effective in providing relief to the target groups than exemptions since there is a lag between payment of the sales tax and receipt of the credit. An exemption provides relief at the time of purchase. In addition, tax credits tend to be more difficult for taxpayers to understand, and the need to file some form of tax return or claim may reduce participation in the program.[18]

States have also enacted a wide range of sales tax exemptions beyond household necessities, ranging from the exemption of certain types of purchasers (e.g., non-profit organizations and governments) to certain types of products (e.g., farm equipment or textbooks). While each exemption no doubt has its merits, their cumulative effect is the substantial erosion of the tax base. Such exemptions can also create equity problems by favoring one type of purchaser over another or one type of product over another. A number of states periodically examine their exemptions (through tax expenditure studies) as a means of assessing their impact and continued necessity.[19]

Interstate Mail Order Sales

One of the most vexing problems facing states is the collection of use tax on interstate mail order or direct marketing transactions. Collection of this tax is important to keep in-state retailers from facing a competitive disadvantage vis-à-vis out-of-state vendors, who are not required to collect state use taxes if their contacts with customers in a state are limited to the use of the U.S. mail and common carriers.[20] The uncollected use tax on mail order sales may total as much as $3 billion annually.[21] States have several options available to close this loophole.

Federal action. In recent years, there have been several efforts to secure federal legislation authorizing states to require direct marketers to collect use taxes on goods shipped into the state. Rep. Jack Brooks (D-Tex.) introduced the most recent bill in 1989.[22] This and other measures encountered opposition from the direct marketing industry. Following the Supreme Court's clear finding of congressional authority in the area (in *Quill Corporation vs. North Dakota*, 1992; see note 19), similar proposals are likely in the new Congress.

Administrative means. States have undertaken a variety of efforts to collect the use tax within the authority available to them under current law. These include:

• Entering into reciprocal agreements to provide for the routine exchange of information on goods shipped into a state to facilitate collection of the tax directly from the consumer.

• Facilitating voluntary payment of use tax by individual customers through the individual income tax system.[23]

• Entering into voluntary arrangements with direct marketers for collection of the tax.

Conclusion

State sales taxes are in need of substantial overhaul if they are to continue to play their traditional role as a workhorse in the state-local revenue system. States must seriously consider expanding the sales tax base, or they are likely to be confronted with the need to continually adjust the tax rate if the sales tax is to continue providing its historical share of state revenues. The taxation of certain service transactions and an examination of current exemptions offer the most likely avenues for revitalizing the sales tax base. Each such move raises serious policy issues and confronts policymakers with trade-offs which at first blush may seem unpalatable. Over the long run, however, significant changes are necessary to preserve a vibrant retail sales tax.

Notes

1. Since 1960, the sales tax has grown from 24 percent to 33 percent of state tax revenues; since 1977 it has risen from 7 percent to 11 percent of local tax revenues as states and localities have begun to diversify the revenue structure and avoid the traditional reliance on the property tax.

2. For more information on the current taxation of services among the states, *see* Federation of Tax Administrators, Sales *Taxation of Services—Who Taxes What?* Research Report 137 (Washington, D.C., April 1991).

3. For thorough reviews of these and other issues, the reader is encouraged to see Federation of Tax Administrators, *Sales Taxation of Services—Who Taxes What?*; Federation of Tax Administrators, Sales Taxation of Services, Research Report 135 (Washington, D.C., October 1990); William Fox and Matthew Murray, "Economic Aspects of Taxing Services," *National Tax Journal* 41, no. 1 (March 1988): 19-36; and Mindy S. Piatoff, "Difficulties in Structuring a Sales Tax on Services, State Tax Notes," State Tax Notes 3, no. 7 (August 17, 1992): 232-240.

4. In some states, business purchases account for as much as 50 percent of all sales tax receipts, with the national average estimated to be 41 percent. *See* Raymond J. Ring, Jr., "The Proportion of Consumers' and Producers' Goods in the General Sales Tax," *National Tax Journal* 42, no. 2 (June 1989), pp. 167-79.

5. *See* for example, John L. Mikesell, "State Sales Tax Policy in a Changing Economy," and Minnesota Department of Revenue, *Model Revenue System for Minnesota* (St. Paul, Minn., July 1992).

6. *See* Walter Hellerstein, "Sales Taxation of Services: An Overview," and William F. Fox, "Sales Taxation of Services: Has Its Time Come?" in William F. Fox, ed., *Sales Taxation: Critical Issues in Policy and Administration*, (Westport, Conn.: Praeger, 1992), pp. 41-50, 51-62.

7. Mikesell, "State Sales Tax Policy."

8. Florida legislation created a broad-based sales tax on services to be effective in mid-1987. Service-sector resistance, led by the advertising industry, resulted in replacement of the potential services taxes with a rate increase on the previous base, before the services taxes went into effect. Massachusetts would have put a broad-based sales tax on business services in effect in 1991, but anti-tax feeling and the belief that some exemptions had occurred because of their industries' political clout led to repeal in 1991 before the new taxes became operative.

9. James Francis, "The Florida Sales Tax on Services: What Really Went Wrong?" discusses the Florida sales tax law and the need to apportion the taxation of certain services. *See also* Massachusetts Department of Revenue, Draft Regulations 830 CMR 64H.6.8, Allocation and Apportionment of the Use of Services, dated November 8, 1990.

10. Empirical studies provide limited evidence that sales taxes affect business activities. William Fox, "Tax Structure and the Location of Economic Activity Along State Borders," National Tax Journal 39, No. 4 (December 1986): 387-401, provides evidence that different sales tax rates along a state's border can cause a significant effect on employment. Bartik, "Small Business Start-Ups in the U.S.: Estimates of the Effects of Characteristics of States," Working Paper No. 87-W15, Nashville: Department of Economics and Business Administration, Vanderbilt

University, 1987, finds that only the differential sales tax rates on machinery and equipment were a significant variable in his equations determining business location.

11. For a state-by-state overview of service taxation by type of service, *see* Federation of Tax Administrators, "FTA Updates Sales Taxation of Services Survey," *Tax Administrators News* 56, no. 11 (November 1992): 126ff.

12. Currently 26 states exempt food for off-premises consumption, six states exempt purchases of some or all clothing, 44 exempt prescription drugs, 26 exempt residential electric and gas utilities, and seven states exempt nonprescription drugs. *See* generally, Advisory Commission on Intergovernmental Relations, *Significant Features of Fiscal Federalism: 1992* (Washington. D.C., February 1992), Vol. 1, pp. 89-91.

13. *See* Steven D. Gold, "Simplifying the Sales Tax: Credits or Exemptions?" and Richard F. Dye and Therese J. McGuire, "Expanding the Sales Tax Base: Implications for Growth and Stability," in William F. Fox, ed., *Sales Taxation: Critical Issues in Policy and Administration*, pp. 157-168 and pp. 169-176.

14. Arturo Pérez, "Food Purchases Add Weight to State Sales Tax Collections," *The Fiscal Letter* XIV, no. 3 (May/June 1992): 4-5.

15. A recent study of Connecticut's food and clothing exemption, for example, estimated the tax relief attributable to the exemption at $500 per household, only 4.6 percent of which went to low-income households. Source: KPMG Policy Economics Group, *Report on the Connecticut Sales and Use Tax, Prepared for the State of Connecticut Task Force on State Tax Revenues*, January 11, 1991.

16. Richard Pomp, "Simplicity and Complexity in the Context of a State Tax System," in Steven D. Gold, ed., *Reforming State Tax Systems*, pp. 134-135. Here the author reports on difficulties in complying with a New York State exemption for nonprescription drugs. One test of purchasing the identical basket of goods in seven different pharmacies resulted in a different amount of tax with each purchase.

17. U.S. Advisory Commission on Intergovernmental Relations, *Significant Features of Fiscal Federalism—1992*.

18. For a more complete discussion, *see* Steven D. Gold, "Simplifying the Sales Tax: Credits or Exemptions?" pp. 157-168.

19. A non-inclusive list of states involved in tax expenditure analysis includes Virginia, Washington, New York, Texas, and Florida. For further discussion, *see* Richard D. Pomp, "State Tax Expenditure Budgets—And Beyond," in Steven D. Gold, ed., *The Unfinished Agenda for State Tax Reform*, pp. 65-82.

20. In *Quill Corp. vs. North Dakota*, U.S.S.C. Doc. No. 91-194, the U.S. Supreme Court reaffirmed its 1967 holding in *National Bellas Hess vs. Illinois Department of Revenue*, 386 U.S. 753 (1967), that a mail-order company must have a presence beyond communication with customers by means of the U.S. mail and common carriers before incurring responsibility to collect use tax. Solicitation of orders by catalog and delivery of goods by common carrier or the mails does not establish sufficient presence to require use tax collection. In *Quill*, however, the court further held that the Due Process clause of the U.S. Constitution does not bar the state from exercising jurisdiction over such a marketer and made it clear that Congress has authority to require direct marketers to collect state use taxes.

21. U.S. Advisory Commission on Intergovernmental Relations, *State Taxation of Interstate Mail-Order Sales: Revised Revenue Estimates, 1990-92* (Washington, D.C., 1991).

22. H.R. 2230 introduced in the 101st Congress.

23. A number of states enable taxpayers to remit use tax as part of their individual income tax return. In Maine, a taxpayer must make an entry as to use tax due, or the state automatically assesses an amount equal to .04 percent of adjusted gross income to the taxpayer.

CHAPTER 13
INDIVIDUAL INCOME TAXES

In a tax system that is often criticized as regressive and failing to keep pace with underlying economic changes, the personal income tax in most states retains some progressivity and elasticity. It is not as threatened with obsolescence as the retail sales tax and the corporation income tax.

Nonetheless, as chapter 10 indicates, the state personal income tax faces problems. In addition to addressing those problems, many states should consider increasing their reliance on the personal income tax because of its many desirable characteristics—its broad base, flexibility, potential for offsetting the regressive effects of other state and local taxes, and its productivity—which help it measure up well to the criteria for a good revenue system discussed in chapter 3. Following are some of the options available to the states in evaluating potential changes in the tax.

Conformity of State Personal Income Tax Bases to the Federal Base
There are many reasons for states to conform their personal income tax base to the federal income tax, but doing so does limit states' policy options and at least in the short run can move the state income tax out of state control. The federal government largely defines the base of the tax, and will continue to do so because of its domination of the tax. States conform to the base to provide consistency in the treatment of income, accommodate their taxpayers by simplifying compliance, and facilitate administration. In addition to the points listed above, these are further characteristics of state income taxes that put them into accord with the principles of a quality revenue system.

Consequently, decoupling state income taxes from the federal base is not a practical option, and states that do not conform to a federal starting point should consider doing so. Furthermore, if states consider decoupling from any current or future federal provisions, they should carefully weigh the impact on the taxpayers' costs in complying with the change and the administrative burdens and risks such a move might entail.

But conformity carries its costs, adding an element of unpredictability to the tax base because of the federal propensity to tinker with the income tax. States now face the possibility of significant changes in the federal personal income tax. Several recent analyses have recommended that the federal income tax be revised to reduce its impact on savings and investment and to focus the tax more fully on consumption.[1] Such a move could significantly affect the productivity and the distribution of the income tax burden and would require a response on the part of states.[2] States would also have to revise their income tax codes in response to another proposal, integration of the federal corporate and personal income taxes.[3] Finally, the federal government may finance health care reform by limiting the deductibility of the health insurance premiums for both employers and employees.[4] Doing so would raise the issue of the appropriate state response to federal base broadening designed specifically for the federal purpose of financing health care reform.

Preferential Treatment in State Tax Codes

Many states have individually adopted exemptions, exclusions, and deductions not found in the federal tax code. Given the relatively low rates of state income taxes in comparison with federal rates, it is unlikely that these preferences have a significant impact in promoting or discouraging the economic behavior they are aimed at. It might be a good idea to eliminate them in order to protect the state tax base; at the very least, states should review whether such incentives have the impact they were intended to have.

A state deduction for federal taxes paid is particularly difficult to defend. It forces nominal rates to be higher in order to raise a given amount of revenue, which is potentially a disincentive to economic development. The deduction also makes the state income tax appear more progressive than it is, and shifts the burden of the state tax to lower-income households whenever the progressivity of the federal tax is increased. Another matter ripe for reconsideration is the state income tax treatment of elderly citizens and retirement income generally. Given the aging of the population and the potential structural and revenue consequences of such measures, it is not unreasonable to ask why income tax preferences should be awarded on the basis of age without consideration of income level. Equity considerations alone suggest a review of such policies.[5]

Progressivity

The graduated income tax is the one weapon in the state tax arsenal that is progressive in its incidence across income classes. For that reason, states should evaluate any changes in their income taxes with an eye on how the changes affect the entire state and local tax structure, not just the personal income tax. The income tax is probably the best vehicle available for offsetting the regressivity of property and sales taxes. If the general incidence of state and local taxes is a concern, state governments can consider improving the progressivity of the individual income tax.

A variety of techniques are available, among them:

• Increased graduation of rates, that is, higher rates for higher income taxpayers.

• Increased personal exemption allowances and standard deductions, which shelter income against taxation, but which somewhat favor higher-income taxpayers over lower-income taxpayers if the rate structure is graduated.

• Conversion of some exemptions and deductions to credits against tax liability, which does not favor higher income taxpayers over lower income taxpayers.

• Elimination of exclusions or deductions that favor higher income taxpayers, or phasing them out as income rises.

In many cases, greater conformity to the federal tax base (e.g., starting with taxable income or piggybacking on federal liability) would also increase the progressivity of the state tax.[6] Higher nominal rates, however, may not be an attractive option, since they may discourage efforts to increase earnings, and may discourage state economic development.

Dealing with Mobile Taxpayers

A current problem in state income tax administration is dealing with mobile taxpayers—those who live in one state and work in one or more other states, or people who leave a state when they retire and receive retirement income originating in their original state if the state to which they have moved does not have an income tax. There is no serious question about a state's right to collect income tax from an out-of-state resident on income that arises in the state; that power is well-established. At issue instead are the compliance difficulties facing those who have to file returns in various states, and the difficulty of efficient and even-handed enforcement.

Complex issues do not have simple answers. A working spirit of interstate cooperation is a good place to begin dealing with such problems. Some techniques are:

• *De minimis* thresholds or other limitations which reduce the number of taxpayers affected

• Uniform rules for allocation to avoid double taxation

• "Composite" returns allowing a number of people to file a single return

• Mechanisms allowing individuals to meet filing requirements in several states with a single return.

Conclusion

Besides their importance as a source of revenue, state income taxes are important for the ways they can reduce the regressivity of state and local tax burdens. The problems of the state personal income tax are entirely manageable in comparison with those of sales and business taxes. The means for dealing with most existing problems are at hand, and call for minor adjustments rather than sweeping change. The largest issues are only potential: the issues that would arise in another round of federal revision of the national income tax.

Notes

1. Senator Sam Nunn and Senator Pete Domenici, *The Strengthening of America Commission: First Report* (Washington, D.C.: Center for Strategic and International Studies, 1992), pp 96-99.

2. Whether the states would be required to scrap their current systems and adapt the new federal base would depend on the nature of the federal tax, particularly the continued availability of information on currently deductible expenses. Such an income tax might also raise serious allocation problems regarding multistate investments.

3. U.S. Department of Treasury, *Report of the Treasury on Integration of the Individual and Corporate Tax Systems—Taxing Business Income Once* (Washington, D.C., January 1992) and U.S. Department of Treasury, *A Recommendation for Integration of the Individual and Corporate Tax Systems* (Washington, D.C., December 11, 1992).

4. National Governors' Association, "State and Local Government and Business Leaders Support Managed Competition Approach to Health Care," news release, December 15, 1992.

5. *See* Keith Carlson, "State Income Tax Treatment of Senior Citizens Changing," *State Tax Notes* 2, no. 6 (February 10, 1992): 192-200, a discussion of the intragenerational and intergenerational equity effects of state tax preferences for the elderly.

6. For examples and details of ways to increase the progressivity of state personal income taxes, *see* Iris J. Lav, *Taxing the Top: Strategies for Increasing State Income Tax Revenue Without Changing Tax Rates* (Washington, D.C.: Center on Budget and Policy Priorities, 1993). Although Lav's emphasis is on revenue increases, many of the state examples and proposals in her study are readily adaptable to increasing the progressivity of a state income tax with offsetting revenue reductions if desirable.

CHAPTER 14
THE CORPORATE INCOME TAX

In addition to any specific substantive changes in business tax policy that states might consider is the need to change the policymaking process itself. Given the rapidly changing character of business enterprise, outlined in chapters 6 and 7, individual states can no longer afford to make business tax policy entirely on their own. In order to preserve a viable, fair system of business taxation, states have to cooperate in formulating policy, drafting laws, and administering their business taxes.[1] The arguments for such cooperation are both practical and political.

Practical Needs

First, it has been shown already that if the technical details of state business taxes are not coordinated, there is a risk of creating inequities among taxpayers because substantial amounts of income and transactions legally escape taxation. Cooperative interstate policy development with input from business taxpayers is also the best way to prevent the adoption of policies that would lead to multiple taxation, which businesses understandably oppose.[2]

Second, unless Congress repeals P.L. 86-272 (see Glossary) and overturns *Bellas Hess*, the state revenue losses from these limits on state taxing authority can be mitigated only by interstate cooperation. States could deal with P.L. 86-272's contribution to the creation of "nowhere income" by agreeing to eliminate from apportionment factors a corporation's sales and payroll in states in which the corporation cannot be taxed.[3] States could respond to *Bellas Hess* with an interstate compact providing that the states in which interstate sales originate would impose sales taxes on outbound sales and that the consequent revenue would be distributed among the members of the compact (see chapter 17).[4]

The final practical argument for greater interstate cooperation is economy of effort, which would benefit both state government and taxpayers. States face similar needs as they study the industries, businesses, and transactions they seek to tax. It does not make sense for 50 separate legislative or tax department staffs to study, for example, the telecommunications industry to devise a definition of interstate telecommunications services to use in the sales tax law. Not only would this squander state resources, but it would be likely to produce 50 slightly different definitions without any real policy differences, forcing all affected taxpayers to track different definitions to comply with the law. A common effort in writing tax law, therefore, benefits both state government and taxpayers. If greater uniformity among state tax laws can be achieved, the feasibility and cost-effectiveness of a variety of cooperative administrative mechanisms, such as joint auditing, centralized registration, and centralized tax return filing, would also be greatly enhanced.

Political Realities

There also are compelling political arguments for interstate cooperation.

First, cooperation among states can make it politically easier for each of them to act. Any significant tax policy change creates winners and losers, with the losers far more likely than the winners to mobilize in response to a proposed change. Especially when proposed changes affect interstate operations or transactions, business taxpayers will make forceful arguments about adverse effects on economic development and the potential for double taxation. These arguments would be less credible if states developed and enacted tax policy changes jointly. It is possible, for example, that the outcome of Florida's attempt to expand the sales to services would have been different if, say, 10 states had cooperated to develop the law and regulations and had enacted it at the same time. Similarly, the opposition that any separate entity corporation income tax state will encounter in proposing to change to waters-edge combination (see Glossary under *combined reporting*) would weaken if the other separate entity states agreed to a simultaneous switch (see Glossary). Cooperation is the best route to preserving viable state business taxation.

Second, cooperation could provide a forum for addressing the issue of interstate tax competition. Many state policymakers agree that state tax competition is so out of control that it threatens state tax bases.

States are unlikely to negotiate a "disarmament" treaty and forswear using tax incentives to attract major business developments, but there may be hope for enough "arms control" to limit the size and number of weapons in the economic development arsenal. For example, states could agree to restore uniformity to their corporation income tax apportionment rules and depreciation schedules and to compete only with lower corporate tax rates or relatively more visible investment tax credits. If an appropriate forum existed to negotiate such agreements, some of the "beggar-thy-neighbor" aspects of tax competition could be avoided.

Forestalling federal pre-emption is the third political reason for greater state cooperation (see chapter 8). If the states do not achieve greater uniformity in tax laws, they are likely to confront a stream of pre-emptive federal legislation. When there is a need to enact new taxes or revise existing law, coordinated state responses might work to prevent the political isolation that would tempt adversely affected taxpayers to seek federal pre-emption.

Policy options. The corporate income tax is the major direct tax that state governments impose upon business enterprises.[5] Although the corporate income tax produces only about 8 percent of state tax revenue on average, few states could afford to dispense with it. Restructuring the tax could make it more productive without a change in rates, help stabilize its revenue yield, and reduce the disparities among different industries and forms of business organization.

The transfer pricing issue. Nearly all states with a corporate income tax conform the base closely to the federal definition of taxable income. Conformity simplifies taxpayer compliance and enforcement of the tax. However, state conformity to the federal definition of U.S.-source income of multinational corporations is causing an intolerable drain on state revenues because of the federal government's inability to prevent improper transfer pricing.

Some states once prevented such tax base erosion by using the worldwide unitary combination method (see Glossary). It makes transfer prices between commonly owned U.S. and foreign corporations engaged in a unitary business irrelevant. The combined income of the corporations after inter-company charges are eliminated becomes the tax base for apportionment to the states.[6] Pressure from corporations, foreign governments, and the federal government in the 1980s led all states but Alaska to eliminate mandatory use of worldwide unitary combination.

Taken together, the corporate income tax states may be losing billions of dollars each year because of international transfer pricing. They must act collectively to put pressure on the federal government to devise an effective solution to the problem and to do so by accurately measuring U.S.-source income, to which state corporate tax bases are tied.[7] Some potential federal solutions, like changes in foreign tax credit rules, would provide no state benefits.[8] Others, such as alternative minimum taxes, would require states to pass conforming legislation which would be likely to meet substantial opposition.[9] The states stopped using worldwide combination in exchange for a commitment from the federal government to increase its protection of their tax bases, and the states should make sure the commitment is fulfilled.[10] At the same time, the states should only support federal approaches that do not discriminate against foreign-based companies.

Comprehensive waters-edge combined reporting. The states have it in their power to protect themselves from improper domestic income shifting. More than one-third of the states that have a corporate income tax have done so by requiring corporations formed in the United States to calculate their taxes on the basis of unitary combined reporting. The other corporate income tax states should consider the advantages of combined reporting—both those that now prohibit it and those that allow its use only in limited circumstances.

Waters-edge combined reporting (see Glossary under *combined reporting*) should be considered, not only because of the problems associated with separate-entity accounting, but also because of two 1992 Supreme Court decisions that prohibit approaches states have been using to compensate for some of the revenue shifting to which separate entity accounting is vulnerable.[11]

Special apportionment rules for service-oriented industries. The shortcomings of the Uniform Division of Income for Tax Purposes Act (UDITPA) have led many states to devise special apportionment formulas for some service industries, like broadcasting, banking, and interstate transportation. Special rules are needed, but their adoption by only a limited number of states has produced the risk of creating "nowhere income," double taxation, or both, and of inviting federal pre-emption. These considerations should push states toward cooperation in developing apportionment rules that all or most of them can adopt.

Achieving significant uniformity in state apportionment methods will require a reasonable balance between recognition of the marketing and production activities of businesses. As discussed above, UDITPA's rules for attributing receipts from services and intangibles have a heavy bias toward states which are the location of production. Many of the special apportionment formulas for service industries, on the other hand, are intended to boost the apportionment of income for the states where service companies' customers are located. However, there is a need to develop generic rules to apportion income from services and intangibles, because many of the industry distinctions upon which the special formulas are based are artificial and threaten to tilt the competitive playing field unfairly.

Not all of the possible approaches to apportioning a greater share of business income to market states are workable. For example, attributing the sales of services to the state where they are "consumed" can be difficult, if not impossible, if the consumer is a multistate business. Where is the service of providing advice on business takeovers made use of when the recipient of the advice and the takeover targets both are multistate businesses? Such difficulties argue for greater interstate cooperation in developing apportionment rules because the more states that are involved, the greater the likelihood that all the potential problems will be identified.

Industry-specific taxes. States should examine their business taxes to avoid applying different tax policies to industries and businesses that compete in the marketplace. Many states single out particular industries for special tax provisions—financial institutions, insurance companies, and telephone and electric power companies. At one time, special taxation was coupled with regulation of such industries' activities and pricing, particularly for companies that were allowed to monopolize a service for some geographic area. Because many such regulations have been loosened or abolished, the special tax provisions may have grown outdated and can in fact produce divergent tax burdens for businesses that compete in a given market.

Telecommunications and financial services are two good examples of industries for which a reexamination of state tax policy may be warranted. The rapid evolution of services and the increase in competition can make old tax policies inappropriate. States should consider treating telecommunications companies like any other corporation for tax purposes, which may involve the substitution of corporate income and property taxes for gross receipts taxes. Similarly, states should provide comparable, if not identical, tax treatment for regulated and nonregulated financial institutions.[12]

Partnerships, S-corporations, and limited liability companies. The federal tax code recognizes several forms of "pass-through entities"—businesses that are usually not taxed directly, but whose income and corresponding deductions are passed directly to the owners of the business and taxed on the owners' tax returns. "S-corporations" are regular corporations with a very limited number of owners who make a federal election to be treated as a pass-through entity. General partnerships are businesses whose owners all participate in the management of the business and who are each personally liable for the debts of the business. Limited partnerships have a special class of owners, "limited partners," who are not liable for the debts of the business but may not participate in its management. Very recently, states have imported a foreign form of business organization, the "limited liability company" (LLC). An LLC provides the major advantage of operating as a corporation (limited liability for all of the owners), while avoiding under IRS rules both the corporate income tax and the many restrictions placed on S-corporations and partnerships.[13]

Most states have conformed to the federal "pass-through" treatment of S-corporations, general partnerships, and limited partnerships. As LLCs become more common, economic competitiveness arguments will likely pressure most states to authorize their creation and provide them with pass-through treatment as well. Such conformity simplifies taxpayer compliance and administrative enforcement, but it has its price.

State conformity to federal pass-through treatment of S-corporations, partnerships, and LLCs poses serious enforcement difficulties if the entity does business in more than one state and/or if its owners live in more than one state. States have administrative difficulty in taxing the income passed through to owners who reside in other states, income which the states may tax under the source principle of taxation. States in which owners live have, as one example, the problem of determining whether credits claimed for taxes paid in other states have been properly calculated.

A model law has been devised to deal with multistate S-corporations, and some states have systems under which partnerships file returns on behalf of their non-resident members. Cost-effective enforcement remains a problem, however. For example, a limited partnership can have thousands of owners, each of whose share of annual income may be only a few hundred dollars. More generally, most state revenue agencies simply have not had enough resources to devote to ensuring that passed-through income is reported and taxed properly.

Until states are able to devote sufficient personnel and computer system development to enforcement of existing law, they should consider decoupling from conformity with federal pass-through treatment and impose either their regular corporate income tax or a special entity-level tax on such business organizations.

Conclusion

Improved interstate cooperation on business tax policy is essential if states are to address issues of equity and tax base erosion. This is not a proposal to shift more of the tax burden to business. Instead, this point recognizes that changing patterns of economic activity and business organization have made much current tax law fail in reaching original intentions. Some business organizations find legal advantages in existing laws that are unavailable to their competitors. Some forms of such inequities may lead to further federal intervention in state tax policy. Existing problems can be addressed, but states may fail to do so individually. Greater cooperation is needed.

Notes

1. In the context of this argument, sales and use taxes should be viewed as part of a state's business tax structure, because a substantial share of the taxes is paid by business, and because businesses collect them. The arguments here generally apply to the multistate issues in personal income taxation and property taxation as well.

2. The current efforts of the Multistate Tax Commission's member states and the state of New York to reach a compromise with each other and with the banking industry on ways to tax income from interstate banking is a good example of the desirable process. The banking industry played an important role in organizing this process. *See* Jack Hodges and Victor Zammit, "Recent Developments Regarding the Proposed Multistate Tax Commission Financial Regulation," *State Tax Notes* 2, no. 16 (April 20, 1992): 551-555.

3. The technical description of such a change is the substitution of a throwout provision for the current throwback rule. It would have the effect of distributing the profits on such interstate sales to all of the states in which the corporation is taxable in proportion to the remaining apportionment factors (see Glossary).

4. States could also agree to share information from audits of businesses to identify customers in other states who purchased expensive items. *See* David Doerr, "BOE [Board of Equalization] Planning Major Use Tax Collections Effort," *State Tax Notes* 3, no. 14 (October 5, 1992): 478, for a report on such an agreement initiated by California. States could adopt a uniform law to impose a sales tax on outbound interstate shipments. *See* Paull Mines, "Transactional Taxation of Interstate Commerce," *Multistate Tax Commission Review* V, no. 1 (December 1992): 19-23.

5. In some states the corporate income tax technically is a corporate franchise tax measured by net income. Some states, including Texas, levy significant corporate franchise taxes based upon the value of the business rather than its income; a recent amendment to the Texas tax requires corporations to pay the greater of the value-based franchise tax or a taxed on "earned surplus," which is essentially profits plus executive compensation. The state of Washington levies a broad-based gross receipts tax rather than a corporate net income tax, and a number of states substitute gross receipts taxes for income taxes for certain industries.

6. The elimination includes payments attributable to intercompany intangibles such as interest on loans made by a parent corporation to a subsidiary, dividends paid by a wholly owned subsidiary to a parent corporation, and royalties paid by one subsidiary to another for the right to use a patent or trademark.

7. A discussion of the effectiveness of the various potential solutions to the problem is beyond the scope of this discussion; see the Glossary for formula-apportionment based approaches.

8. The profits of the foreign subsidiaries of U.S.-based multinational corporations are taxed by the U.S. when they are repatriated in the form of dividends to their parent companies. However, a credit against this U.S. tax is provided (with limitations) for foreign taxes already paid on the subsidiary's profits out of which the dividend was paid. Rather than adjusting incorrect transfer prices to increase U.S. source income, the federal government could reduce the credit for foreign taxes. This would not benefit the states, which do not grant a foreign tax credit.

9. James E. Wheeler and Richard P. Weber, "A New Minimum Tax as a Solution to Inbound and Outbound Section 482 Problems, the Complexity of the Current, and the Need for More Tax Revenues," *Tax Notes* 49, no. 7 (November 12, 1990): 793-798.

10. *See* Dan R. Bucks, "Will the Emperor Discover He Has No Clothes Before the Empire is Sold?" *National Tax Journal* 44, no. 3 (September 1991): 311-314, for a discussion of the state-federal relationship on this issue.

11. Paull Mines, "Supreme Court Decisions in Allied-Signal and Kraft Push States to Consider Combined Reporting," *Multistate Tax Commission Review* V, no. 1 (December 1992): 1.

12. *See* U.S. Advisory Commission on Intergovernmental Relations, *State Taxation of Banks: Issues and Options* (December, 1989) and ACIR, *State Taxation of Telecommunications*, forthcoming.

13. Scott Smith, "Limited Liability Companies: What Are They and What Are Their Implications for State Taxation?" *Multistate Tax Commission Review* V, no. 1 (December 1992): 1.

CHAPTER 15
THE VALUE ADDED TAX

The value added tax (VAT) is a broad-based business tax which offers some advantages over existing direct taxes on business such as the corporate income tax and sales taxes and could be used to supplement or replace these state revenue sources. The VAT is often discussed in state tax studies for that reason. Its advantages are substantial, at least in theory. Its unfamiliarity to most Americans, policymakers' preference for limited changes within the existing tax system over substantial reform, and the shifting of tax burdens that would follow adoption all present significant obstacles to state governments' adoption of the VAT.

The VAT in some form is a national tax in Canada, Japan, and the European Economic Community countries. Only Michigan currently has a tax that approximates a VAT. Recent years have seen new interest in the VAT among state policymakers, although so far the interest has not induced any state to add a VAT.[1] Among the features that explain this interest are the way that a VAT could replace a number of existing business taxes with one tax, could resolve a number of the problems related to apportionment, application and equity that characterize current business taxation, could substitute for the extension of the sales tax to business services while preventing pyramiding, and could produce a substantial amount of revenue while maintaining a low rate.

Definition

A VAT is collected from businesses. It is applied to goods and services at each stage in their production and distribution, on the amount of value that a processor or supplier adds. There are two forms of value added tax. In one, the state in which value is produced collects the tax. The other is a type of general consumption tax, with only the state where final household consumption occurs collecting the tax. The first type of VAT, the "operational VAT," is based on the results of the taxpayer's overall operations. The second type of VAT, the "transaction-based VAT," is based on records of individual transactions, both sales and purchases.[2]

Operational VAT

The operational VAT is levied directly on value added, defined as the taxpayer's gross receipts minus the cost of the taxpayer's purchases from other firms. The operational VAT is the type used by Michigan and was given constitutional approval in the 1991 U.S. Supreme Court decision in *Trinova Corp. vs. Michigan Department of Treasury.*

The taxpayer—the business firm—calculates value added in one of two ways, as determined by tax law:

(1)   By subtracting from its gross receipts all of its purchases from other firms (the *subtractive approach*) or

(2)   By summing up payrolls, rent, interest, and profits (the *additive approach*).

Either way, the size of the tax base is the same. The choice is largely settled by questions of ease of administration and taxpayer compliance.

If the business operates in several states, it apportions a share of its total value added to the taxing state using the same type of apportionment methods states now require for corporate income tax purposes. The business applies the tax rate to the value added attributable to the taxing state and pays the resulting tax amount.

Partly because it includes payrolls in the tax base, an operational VAT is inherently a more stable source of revenue than income or profits-based taxes, meaning that collections do not fall as sharply in a recession. This stability is of course a two-edged sword, since a company's tax payments do not fall as fast when profits turn down.[3] It may be argued, however, that the benefits governments provide business do not disappear when the business becomes unprofitable and that, therefore, choosing value added rather than profit as a tax base is more consistent with the benefits principle underlying direct state taxation of businesses.[4]

A VAT—in its operational form—may be simpler and certainly is no more complex for a state to administer than a corporate income tax and can replace a variety of other business taxes since it can be applied to all types of businesses regardless of the nature of the business or its organization. The Michigan Single Business Tax replaced the corporate profits tax, franchise tax, business intangibles tax, property tax on inventory, the financial institutions tax, the insurance company privilege fee, and the savings and loan company privilege fee.

An operational VAT is also more neutral with regard to business decision making than other business taxes. It can readily be configured to allow producers to deduct capital expenses from their tax base, treating a capital expenditure no differently from an expenditure for raw materials.[5] Unlike the corporate income tax, it is not tied to any form of business organization and provides no incentive to adopt any particular form of organization. Exemptions for small businesses for reasons of simplicity of compliance and administration can be implemented through a variable exemption that vanishes as a firm's assets increase.[6]

Since its base encompasses the total value of production occurring in a state, the tax base for an apportioned VAT is very broad, making it possible for a low rate to produce large amounts of revenue. For example, a VAT with no exemptions or credits and a rate of 1 percent would have produced $1.3 billion in collections in Texas in fiscal year 1986, which can be compared with the $1.05 billion that each penny of the sales tax rate produced that year.[7] This productive capacity has led to recommendations for the use of a federal VAT to fund health care reform, and the states' adoption of a VAT on a base common to them all as a means of meeting the fiscal needs the 1990s will bring.[8]

An operational VAT has drawbacks relative to the state corporate income tax for which it is a likely replacement, however. Many people believe that the operational VAT will be passed through into the price of products, making it regressive, like other taxes on consumption. (Others believe that the operational VAT, such as levied by Michigan, may not be regressive and may have an impact or incidence similar to current corporate income and business property taxes.) Critics also charge that the true cost of the VAT is hidden in the price of goods or services, so that the public is unaware of the amount of tax being charged, an objection that can, of course, be made about other taxes paid by businesses that may be passed on to consumers.

Businesses whose profitability is weak will find an operational VAT more oppressive than profitable businesses will, since the liability a VAT imposes is related to payroll as well as profits. Indeed, even businesses operating at a loss will be liable for VAT. Those who feel that some measure of ability to pay should be a consideration in business taxes may find a VAT objectionable.

Transaction-based VAT

The transaction-based VAT is the form used by the European Economic Community countries. No state has adopted this form of the VAT. The most common form of the transaction-based VAT is the invoice-credit VAT. Under this tax, all businesses charge tax on all of their sales, and the tax is shown on all invoices or cash register receipts, like the retail sales tax. The tax is transformed from a gross receipts tax into a value added tax by the provision of a credit for the VAT the business paid on its purchases from suppliers.

The invoice-credit or transaction-based VAT is very different from the operational VAT because of the way it operates in an interstate context. No tax is charged on interstate sales, but the interstate seller still obtains a refund of taxes paid on inputs. The effect is that only the state where the final retail sale takes place collects the tax. (Recall that under the operational VAT the tax is collected by the state(s) where the value is contributed.) In this respect, the invoice-credit VAT is quite similar to sales and use taxes, which is why it has been advocated as a replacement for existing sales and use taxes.

Substituting an invoice-credit VAT for existing state sales taxes has the potential to solve two major current problems in sales taxation. First, it would be perhaps the most direct means of achieving comprehensive taxation of services. By their nature, transactional VATs are based on all transactions being taxable in the first instance. There is no need to distinguish a "retail sale" from a "sale for resale" as under existing state sales taxes. Indeed, a transactional VAT could not operate effectively without including services.

Second, an invoice-credit VAT has major advantages over the sales tax in its ability to prevent tax pyramiding without either imposing undue burdens on sellers or opening the door to sales tax evasion by purchasers. The invoice-credit VAT eliminates pyramiding, because businesses may claim a credit for all VAT paid on their purchases of inputs. The solution to the pyramiding problem under existing sales taxes—simply exempting business purchases of inputs—is hard to administer and subject to abuse. Perhaps the only way to significantly reduce pyramiding without increasing the costs of compliance or the inducements for tax evasion is to require businesses to charge tax on all of their sales and then put the onus on the purchaser to claim (and document its right to) a refund. This is precisely how the invoice-credit VAT operates.

One major problem with adoption by an individual state of an invoice-credit VAT is that there is a significant question of its constitutionality. Any state that adopts a credit-invoice VAT would risk having a major revenue source declared unconstitutional. The constitutional question arises because the VAT frees any product produced wholly in the state from any pyramiding effect. However, the prices of products imported into a state (for example, engines that would be components of cars assembled in-state) would be likely to include some pyramiding. Unless the state allows an in-state purchaser to claim a credit for sales taxes imposed by another state on inputs, the state would run the risk of unconstitutional discrimination against interstate commerce. Even if such claims were allowed, it would be very difficult for taxpayers to calculate the amount accurately and, in any case, states would be reluctant to allow such vendor credits because of the difficulty of auditing the claims.

A second disadvantage of the invoice-credit VAT vis-à-vis the sales tax is that it might require more frequent and thorough auditing of businesses than is necessary to enforce sales taxes. Under current sales taxes, states can limit audits of wholesalers and manufacturers, since most of their sales are exempt. Even if a state were to expand its sales tax to services in a major way, service businesses that sell only to other businesses would still need only light audit coverage. Under the invoice-credit VAT, however, all businesses would collect tax on sales and the state would also need to audit claims for credits. Thus, despite the self-enforcing aspects of the invoice-credit VAT, it might pose a larger administrative burden than sales taxes do. The complexities of compliance are a further obstacle to adoption.

Conclusion

Today, most state tax policymakers remain unfamiliar with the value added tax. This unfamiliarity may lead to a tendency to exaggerate its drawbacks. However, the VAT could address several of the major problems of existing state tax systems—the limited sales tax base as it exists in most states, the pyramiding and consequent distortions that would result from extending the sales tax base to business services, the multiplicity of existing business taxes, and the difficulty in adjusting traditional state business taxes to new forms of business production, services, and forms of organization. For all of these reasons, the VAT deserves and is likely to receive greater consideration from policymakers in the future.

Notes

1. The principal source of this discussion of value added tax is Robert D. Ebel's unpublished paper, "State Value Added Taxation" (January, 1993); *see also* Susan M. Banta, Robert D. Ebel, and Steven Galginaitis, "State Value Added Taxation," *Annual Proceedings of the National Tax Association,* 1992.

2. James Francis, "A Closer Look at a State Invoice-Credit VAT," *State Tax Notes* 3, no. 21 (November 30, 1992): 804-809.

3. John Weiferman, "The Value Added Tax: A Background Analysis," in Billy C. Hamilton, ed., *Rethinking Texas Taxes: Final Report of the Select Committee on Tax Equity,* vol. 2, pp. 239-258, p. 253.

4. *See* note 7 in chapter 8.

5. Important variants of the VAT turn upon how capital deductions are allowed. The *income variant* provides for the depreciation of a capital expenditure over a period of years, as do corporate income taxes. The *consumption variant* provides for full deduction of the capital expenditure in the year the expenditure is made. Ebel, "State Value Added Taxation" *see* also Banta, Ebel, and Galginaitis, "State Value Added Taxation."

6. Banta, Ebel, and Galginaitis, "State Value Added Taxation."

7. NCSL calculation based upon Bureau of the Census, *State Government Tax Collections in 1987*, p. 39, and data in Weiferman, "Value Added Tax." The Texas sales tax rate was .04125—ibid., p. 142.

8. Alice M. Rivlin, *Reviving the American Dream: The Economy, the States, and the Federal Government* (Washington, D.C.: The Brookings Institution, 1992), 143–145.

CHAPTER 16
THE PROPERTY TAX

Voter animosity toward the property tax has spurred a shift by states from reliance on the property tax to the income and sales taxes. This shift is not so much the "rebellion" against the property tax that the media portrays as an evolutionary change in American public finance. State tax systems have become more progressive and the disparities between rich and poor local governments have lessened as state-local finance has moved away from the property tax. But shifting the burden to sales and income taxes has exacerbated the fluctuations in states' revenue collections over the economic cycles and has placed new strains on revenue systems.

In 1970, property taxes provided 39.2 percent of state and local tax collections; in 1990, they provided 31 percent, which was slightly up from the years just previous. State and local governments' combined reliance on property taxes has increased slightly in the past few years as the growth in property values in the 1980s has worked through the assessment system to yield higher taxes, and as slow economic growth has reduced the growth rate of state income and sales tax collections. The long-term trend, however, has been away from property taxes, and that is likely to continue. As previously mentioned, state tax limitation initiatives have hit property taxes especially hard.

Any shift away from reliance on property taxes is accompanied by other difficult policy issues:

• Local governments' efforts to share state personal income, sales, and excise tax bases;

• Reassignment of public responsibilities between state and local governments;

• Increased disparities of public resources among local governments, since access to alternatives to property taxes will be distributed evenly.

Thus, in states where the property tax is under threat, it is all the more important for state personal and corporate income taxes and sales taxes to be revised to reflect the modern economy and demography. Decreased reliance on property taxes is usually coupled with the expectation that state government will absorb more local government expenses. Moving away from the property tax puts stress on all other sources of state and local revenue.

While revenue productivity is an important consideration, there are also other reasons that the property tax is an essential component of a tax system intended to comply with the principles of a sound tax system discussed in chapter 3:

- **Stability.** The property tax is an important source of stability in state-local revenue systems during recessions and periods of slow growth. It responds slowly both in periods of economic expansion and in recession, making it the most certain and predictable source of revenues for school districts and local governments.

- **Compliance.** The key elements of the property tax base, namely land and permanent improvements, are immovable and readily assessed. Tax avoidance and other compliance problems are minimized.

- **Local control.** Property taxes are the one local tax revenue source exclusively reserved for local governments. Taxpayers have more direct control over how their tax money is spent.

Despite these advantages, the property tax is unpopular with the electorate and has been a major factor in tax revolts. Taxpayers frequently do not understand the relationship between market value, assessed value, mill levies, and the actual dollar amount of property tax due. Another problem is the lack of horizontal equity, particularly in jurisdictions where reassessment is performed infrequently.

Strengthening the Property Tax

Many of the problems with the property tax, real or perceived, stem from how the property tax is administered. There are several steps states can take to strengthen property tax administration and relieve the property tax burden on the poor and the elderly on fixed incomes.

Administration. States could require assessors to be certified or meet minimum training requirements. States could require all property to be assessed at full market value, in order to minimize taxpayer confusion about how taxes are calculated. States could require administrative equalization to statistically correct for under-valuation by assessors in certain areas. States could penalize jurisdictions that do not keep assessment rolls at full market value; Vermont, for example, withholds school aid to towns that do not maintain their assessment rolls at a minimum of 80 percent of market value. States could also require frequent reassessment of property to keep assessed values current with market conditions.

Targeted tax relief. States could offer deferral programs for low-income elderly homeowners. (Such programs allow the postponement of tax payments until the owner's death or the sale of the property. The amount of the deferral plus interest constitutes a lien on the property.)

These low-cost programs ensure that no poor elderly person would lose a home because of property taxes. States could also target homestead exemption and credit programs more carefully to financial need (see Glossary). Some states give wealthy elderly homeowners tax relief that they do not need or deserve. Property tax relief programs could also be designed so they do not encourage local government spending.

Helping taxpayers understand the property tax. States could use "full disclosure" or "truth-in-taxation" provisions to help taxpayers understand how their property taxes are calculated and where their tax money is going. States could require that property tax notices contain the following information: the market value upon which assessment is based, how the assessed value is calculated, the mill levy for each taxing jurisdiction, the tax money going to each jurisdiction, how to ask questions about the assessment, and how to formally appeal an assessment.

Fiscal disparities. Disparities between property-rich and property-poor jurisdictions are inherent in the property tax system. When states decide that there is a compelling state interest in reducing or eliminating these disparities, as in education funding, equalization is best addressed through redistributive state aid policies. However, there are options available through the property tax system that, although controversial, are currently used by some states.

Arizona, Kansas, Washington, and Wyoming use a statewide property tax to help equalize education funding throughout the state. All property taxpayers in the state pay a certain mill levy to the state, which is redistributed to school districts. Washington's program is most extensive; one-third of all property tax levies go to the state. Variations of a statewide property tax could include a requirement that commercial and industrial property tax revenues go to the state while residential property tax revenues go to the local jurisdiction.

The Minneapolis-St. Paul area has had a regional tax base sharing arrangement since the mid-1970s. A portion of the commercial and industrial property tax base is shared within a seven-county region, while residential property taxes go to the host municipality. This program reduces interjurisdictional competition for business and industry and helps reduce fiscal disparities between cities and suburbs.

Conclusion

Over the long term, state finance has adjusted to a shift away from property taxes as a source of state and local government revenue. Property taxes still produce nearly one-third of all state and local tax collections and are the mainstay of public schools and most local governments. Probably nothing can reverse the dislike Americans have for property taxes, but they remain essential to public finance. It is possible to correct or mitigate problems of equity, administration, and public misunderstanding. Reducing reliance on property taxes strains other tax sources through the demands for greater state aid to local governments, and preserving the role of property taxes helps preserve the control of local governments over their policies and services.

Notes

1. Scott R. Mackey, *State Property Tax Relief Programs for Homeowners and Renters* (Denver, Colo.: National Conference of State Legislatures, 1992).

2. Steven D. Gold and Martha A. Fabricius, *How States Limit City and County Property Taxes and Spending* (Denver, Colo.: National Conference of State Legislatures, 1992).

3. Steven D. Gold, *Reforming State-Local Relations: A Practical Guide* (Denver, Colo.: National Conference of State Legislatures, 1989).

Chapter 17
Preventing Federal Pre-emption Through Joint State Action

Individually, states have difficulty overcoming threats of federal intervention of the kind discussed in chapter 9. Jointly, states can exercise greater power in relation to the federal government. Often the joint exercise of power by states would involve an interstate compact. Interstate compacts do not necessarily require congressional approval. Indeed, the U.S. Supreme Court has established standards for when congressional approval is required and when it is not necessary.[1]

As noted in chapter 14, states could enact interstate compacts or uniform laws that solve at least some of the mail order sales tax problem. Even if all states do not participate, a major portion of the mail order loophole in the sales tax system can be solved. There are ways that states could have worked together to forestall or limit the impact of the 4R Act, and, indeed, joint action by a major group of states to handle certain railroad property tax practices in a uniform manner could still form the basis for addressing the problems created by the Act.

In the area of commuter taxes, states could develop a uniform law on how income taxation of commuters will operate. While the details are different, the states have accomplished a similar task in the business area through the widespread adoption of the Uniform Division of Income for Tax Purposes Act (UDITPA). If a basic legal framework for interstate business income taxation could be adopted, so could a legal framework for interstate personal income taxation.

Sometimes joint state solutions might require a partnership with the federal government. State taxation of retirement income is a case in point. A national solution might be necessary to ensure some uniform taxation of retirement income and a reasonable sharing of the tax revenue among the various states. That solution might involve a partnership with the federal government through the mechanism of an interstate compact that would require congressional approval and federal participation. That partnership could begin, however, with an agreement among a diverse group of states with different and competing interests as to the features of a national system of state retirement income taxation.

The gas guzzler controversy between Maryland and the U.S. government might have developed differently if Maryland, before proceeding into this area, had recruited other states to establish a uniform system of gas guzzler taxes. A group of states could then combine their legal and political power to resist the attempt by the National Highway Traffic Safety Administration to limit the power of the states through regulatory action.

Conclusion

The problems posed by a federal value added tax could be overcome or forestalled if a major group of states enacted a uniform state system of value added taxes by interstate compact. Although the mechanism of raising the revenue would be uniform, each state would use the revenue in the manner they determine to be best for their circumstances. Because of the broad-based character of a value added tax, it would be likely that many states would use this form of taxation to accomplish some reform and replacement of their existing tax structure. States need not sit by idly while the federal government studies a value added tax. States, acting together, could be the vehicle for the implementation of value added taxation in the United States.[2] At the same time, the states that did not agree with this form of taxation would remain free to retain their existing forms of taxation.

States have not fully exploited their opportunities to work together through compacts to control their own tax policy and ward off threats of further federal intervention. Although the creation of compacts is difficult and time-consuming, it may be the most effective way for states to preserve their traditional tax powers and to oppose the extension of federal uniformity over their spheres of power. Even in the absence of compacts, uniform state laws could resolve some existing issues like that of the mail order sales loophole in state sales tax laws.

Notes

1. In general, only interstate compacts that encroach upon or interfere with federal powers require congressional approval. *See* Benjamin J. Jones and Deborah Reuter, "Interstate Compacts and Agreements," *The Book of the States, 1990-91 Edition* (Lexington, Ky.: The Council of State Governments, 1990), p. 565. In the area of state taxation, the U.S. Supreme Court approved the constitutionality of the Multistate Tax Compact, which deals with state taxation of interstate commerce, even though it was not congressionally approved. *See* U.S. Steel Corporation vs. Multistate Tax Commission, 434 U.S. 452 (1978).

2. *See* John A. Miller, "State Adoption of a Value Added Tax: A Desperate Act in Search of the Proper Occasion," Nebraska Law Review 71, no. 1 (1992): 192-208; John A. Miller, "State Administration of a National Sales Tax: A New Opportunity for Cooperative Federalism," *Virginia Tax Review* 9, no. 2 (Fall 1989): 243-271.

GLOSSARY

Apportionment. The process of using a formula to divide the business income (profit or loss) of a multistate business among the states that have jurisdiction to tax that income. *See also* UDITPA, combination, unitary business, and business vs. non-business income.

Bellas Hess. See *National Bellas Hess.*

Business income vs. non-business income. Terms contained in UDITPA to distinguish corporate profits that are subject to apportionment (business income) from items of income that must be "allocated" to a specific state, frequently the state in which the corporate headquarters are located or in which the asset giving rise to the non-business income is managed. UDITPA defines business income as "income arising from transactions and activity in the regular course of the taxpayer's trade or business and includes income from tangible and intangible property if the acquisition, management and disposition of the property constitute integral parts of the taxpayer's regular trade or business operations." UDITPA defines non-business income as "all income other than business income." An example of non-business income would be the capital gain or profit realized on the sale of stock of a company that was purchased as a passive investment and whose operations were never integrated with the operations of the company that purchased the stock. Whether particular items of income that arise from intangible property (e.g., interest, capital gains, dividends, and royalties) constitute business or non-business income is a frequent matter of controversy between taxpayers and state tax officials. *See also* UDITPA, apportionment.

Circuit breaker. A device to prevent property taxes from becoming an unduly large share of income for some specific class of taxpayers, such a low-income people or the elderly. One form provides state personal income tax credits for a portion of the taypayer's property tax liability. Generally such programs are designed to benefit lower-income people more than higher-income people.

Combination/combined reporting versus separate-entity reporting. States use the technique of apportionment to divide the total profits of a multi-state enterprise among the states with jurisdiction to tax those profits. Many states apportion on a *combined reporting basis*, which means that the profits of all the separate legal entities that make up a single "unitary" business (such as a parent corporation and its subsidiaries engaged in a vertically-integrated production process) are added together, and certain payments among the related companies are eliminated.

The denominator of each apportionment factor is the total property, payroll, or sales of the combined enterprise, and the numerator is the in-state property, payroll, or sales of the company whose tax liability is being calculated. Even under combined reporting, tax liability is determined separately for each separate legal entity, but it is determined by apportioning the combined profit of the entire unitary enterprise.

Under *separate entity reporting* (used by slightly more than half of the states with corporate income taxes), the profit reported for each legally distinct corporation is apportioned separately without reference to the combined profit of the overall enterprise. For example, if a retail department store chain with a central purchasing warehouse in one state and stores in five other states chose to incorporate each of those stores as separate subsidiaries, the profits reported by each of the five stores would be apportioned separately.

Under separate entity apportionment, the potential exists for companies to use *transfer pricing* to shift income to minimize state tax liability. In this example, if the warehouse were located in a low tax rate state, it could charge artificially high prices to stores located in high tax rate states to shift the stores' profits into the low tax rate state. Taxing the chain on a combined reporting basis would eliminate the benefit of such transfer pricing, because the warehouse's profit would be combined with the store's profits before the income was apportioned.

Some states that normally require separate entity reporting may authorize tax officials to require combined reporting or permit taxpayers to file on that basis if they can demonstrate that it achieves a more accurate measure of a corporation's earnings in a state. *See also* domestic vs. worldwide vs. water's-edge combined reporting.

Credit (tax). An amount subtracted from total tax liability. A refundable tax credit is paid even if the amount of the credit exceeds the original amount of tax due.

Destination basis. In the context of apportioning interstate corporations' income among states for purposes of calculating tax liabilities, this refers to the rule that sales of *goods* are treated as occurring at the point at which the customer receives the goods. This rule helps enable the state where the customer is located to tax the selling corporation. The rule does not apply (under UDITPA) to sales of *services*.

Domestic vs. worldwide vs. water's-edge combined reporting. Alternative approaches to combined reporting that differ with respect to which legally separate but commonly owned and controlled corporations engaged in a unitary business ("unitary corporations") are combined for purposes of calculating the income subject to tax in a particular state.

Under *domestic combined reporting*, only unitary corporations that are incorporated in the United States are combined.

Under *worldwide combination*, all of the unitary corporations are combined, regardless of whether they are incorporated in the U.S., a U.S. possession, or a foreign country.

Under *water's-edge combination*, only those unitary corporations with substantial U.S. operations are combined; thus, U.S. unitary corporations with 80 percent or more of their property and payroll located abroad usually are not included in the combined report, while foreign unitary corporations with 20 percent or more of their payroll and property in the U.S. usually are included. Within this general categorization of the three approaches, many state-specific variants exist. Most combined-reporting states require or permit domestic combination. California, Montana, and North Dakota require worldwide combination but permit companies to elect water's-edge combination if certain conditions are satisfied. Alaska is the only state that still requires worldwide combination, but only for multinational oil companies. Worldwide combination was required in about a dozen states until the mid 1980s, when they switched to domestic or water's-edge combination or separate entity reporting in response to objections to the practice and pressure from the federal government, foreign governments, and multinational corporations.

Effective tax rate. With the personal income tax, the effective tax rate is the proportion of total income paid. With the property tax, it is the proportion of a property's market value paid in tax.

4-R Act. The Railroad Revitalization and Regulatory Reform Act of 1976. Section 306 of the 4-R Act prohibits state and local governments from taxing railroad property at a higher effective rate than other business property. A series of court decisions interpreting another provision prohibiting "the imposition of any other tax that results in discriminatory treatment" of a railroad have found that the granting of exemptions for types of property that railroads do not own nonetheless constitutes discrimination against railroads. Section 306 of the 4-R Act is unusual in that it provides direct access to federal courts for railroads wishing to challenge state and local tax practices; other aggrieved taxpayers must challenge such practices through established state administrative and judicial appeals procedures, with ultimate recourse to the U.S. Supreme Court. Along with federal court jurisdiction comes the potential for a railroad to obtain an injunction against paying its taxes while the appeal is being heard. Other property taxpayers must generally pay their taxes while the appeal is in process and then obtain a refund if the appeal is successful. The 1987 U.S. Supreme Court decision in the *Burlington Northern* case held that the 4-R Act allows a railroad to bring a challenge to its valuation in federal court.

General revenue. State revenue collections that are not previously designated or earmarked for a specific expenditure. In most states motor fuel taxes are not general revenue because they are designated for highway maintenance and repair. Personal income taxes usually are undesignated and are general revenue.

Horizontal equity. In a tax system horizontal equity means that people of similar means are taxed similarly. (See *vertical equity*.)

Incidence. A reference to the person or persons who ultimately bear the burden of a tax, as opposed to the *impact* of the tax, which refers to the taxpayer who originally pays it and who may pass some or all of the burden to someone else. Someone who rents a dwelling may bear some of the *incidence* of the property tax although the landlord bears the *impact*.

Income elasticity (tax). For a given revenue system, the responsiveness of tax collections to changes in the tax base. For instance, the amount of growth in tax collections that results from growth of the tax base.

Intangibles. Property which does not exist in physical, concrete form, for example, a database (electronic impulses magically stored in a machine).

Marginal rates. The tax rate or rates to which the last dollar of income is subjected.

Market state-oriented taxation. An imprecise term most often used to characterize proposed changes in state tax policy aimed at strengthening the ability of a *market state* to obtain taxing jurisdiction over out-of-state corporations and to boost, relative to the state's current approaches, the share of such a corporation's income that is apportioned to the states in which its customers are located. An example of a proposed change in tax policy that may be so characterized is the proposal to change UDITPA's sales factor attribution rule for sales of services from a "place of performance" basis to a "destination basis." *See also* origin basis vs. destination basis.

Market state. An imprecise term intended to connote a state in which a business has customers but in which the business does not have a substantial physical presence (plant, employees, etc.). The term is sometimes used to characterize a state in general, but with the dispersion of production activity (and manufacturing, in particular) throughout the United States, it is unclear that this usage has general validity. It may have more validity with respect to industries whose production activities remain concentrated in a few states. The majority of states may be meaningfully characterized as "market states" for the banking industry, which is concentrated in New York, San Francisco, Chicago, and a few other financial centers, and for the television broadcasting industry, which is concentrated in New York and California. *See also* market state-oriented taxation.

***National Bellas Hess* decision.** A 1967 U.S. Supreme Court decision, *National Bellas Hess vs. Illinois Dept. of Revenue*, concerning nexus for state use tax purposes. The decision held that a state could not require an out-of-state mail order catalog company to charge the state's use tax on its sales to customers located in the state when the company's only contacts with the customers and the state involved use of the U.S. mail and common carriers. *See also* nexus, *Quill* decision, use tax.

Nexus. A legal term meaning having sufficient "contacts" with a state to be subject to that state's taxing jurisdiction. Whether an out-of-state company "has nexus" in a particular state remains ambiguous in many circumstances because nexus is ultimately defined by the U.S. Supreme Court and many common factual circumstances have never been examined by the Court.

It is well established that if a business located in State A has more than a *de minimis* amount of its property located in State B or its employees regularly enter State B to conduct business, State B has taxing jurisdiction over the company and can require it, for example, to charge sales or use taxes on its sales to customers located in State B and to pay taxes on its profits to State B.

The ambiguity surrounding the existence of nexus generally arises when a business is making sales or earning a profit without any direct physical presence, e.g., by licensing a trademark in exchange for royalties or through the physical presence of third parties who may or may not be considered its agents. Many state officials believe that a "physical presence" standard for establishing nexus is too limited in a world in which an increasing number of services can be provided via telecommunications and would prefer a much broader standard under which nexus would also exist whenever a business purposefully takes advantage of a profit-making opportunity in a state. *See also* Public Law 86-272, *National Bellas Hess* decision, and *Quill* decision.

Nominal tax rate. Tax rates stated by law and applied to a given level of taxable income, or to the assessed value of property. As opposed to effective tax rates.

"Nowhere income." A term used by some tax administrators to refer to corporate profits that are earned in the United States but are not taxed by any state because of limitations on state taxing jurisdiction, the failure of states to coordinate their apportionment rules or to require combined reporting, or state provisions that establish artificial "tax havens" for certain types of income. Tax administrators do not consider profit that is not taxed because it is apportioned to states without corporate income taxes to be "nowhere income" if the apportionment to such states results from good-faith compliance with normal apportionment rules.

Businesses can legally organize their transactions and legal structures to create nowhere income by taking advantage of any or all of the above phenomena, but nowhere income can come into existence without any deliberate action on the part of taxpayers.

Many business representatives deny that the term has any validity and consider its implications pejorative, since non-taxation most often arises from the failure of states to adopt coordinated rules that could prevent it, or from constitutional or statutory limitations on state taxing authority.

A common cause of nowhere income is the non-taxability of a corporation in a state in which it is making substantial sales. Some portion of a corporation's profits will be untaxed if less than 100 percent of its sales can be attributed to the numerators of the sales factors of all of the states in which it is making sales (*see* UDITPA). For example, 50 percent of a corporation's profits will be nowhere income if the corporation has all of its property and payroll in a state that assigns a 50 percent weight to the sales factor but makes all of its sales in states that levy corporate taxes but have no jurisdiction to tax it (e.g., because its activities there are limited to solicitation of sales—see the definition of Public Law 86-272). *See also* UDITPA, throwback rule, apportionment, transfer price, Public Law 86-272.

Origin basis versus destination basis. Imprecise terms which connote aspects of tax policy tending to subject transactions and income to tax in, respectively, the jurisdiction in which the seller/producer is located and the jurisdiction in which the consumer/customer is located. For example, sales and use taxes together operate with a heavy destination orientation, since states generally exempt sales of goods that the seller can demonstrate will be shipped to or consumed in another state and impose use taxes on incoming goods. Sales of goods are treated on a destination basis for corporate income tax apportionment purposes; that is, the receipts from the sale of goods are assigned to the numerator of the sales factor in the state in which the recipient of the goods is located. In contrast, sales of services are usually assigned to the sales factor numerator of the state in which the majority of the "costs of performance" of the services are incurred, an "origin basis" attribution rule.

Own-source revenue. Revenue a government raises by means of its own legislation or other action, as opposed to grants-in-aid or transfers from another government. State taxes are an own-source revenue for the state that collects them, as opposed to federal Medicaid reimbursements to the state.

Progressivity. The degree to which a tax that imposes a proportionately heavier burden on high income people than on low income people. The federal personal income tax is generally regarded as a progressive tax.

Proportional (tax). A tax that imposes the same burden as a share of income on all taxpayers. A state income tax set at 2 percent of taxable income for all taxpayers would be proportional in terms of taxable income.

Public Law 86-272. A federal law enacted in 1959 that limits the jurisdiction of states to subject out-of-state corporations to their corporate income taxes. P.L. 86-272 provides that a state may not subject an out-of-state corporation to its corporate tax if the corporation's only in-state activity is the solicitation of orders for tangible personal property, which orders are approved out of state and fulfilled by shipment from out-of-state locations. P.L. 86-272 sets a corporate income tax nexus threshold that is more restrictive than that established by U.S. Supreme Court interpretation of the constitutional limits of state corporate income tax jurisdiction, since the regular presence of even a single salesman in a state would establish constitutional nexus but is "protected" by P.L. 86-272 (assuming that the salesman's activities are limited to "solicitation of orders"). P.L. 86-272 does not limit state corporate income tax jurisdiction over out-of-state companies that may be selling services, leasing property, licensing intangibles, etc. in a state; nexus in these circumstances is determined by reference to constitutional principles. *See also* nexus.

Quill decision. A 1992 U.S. Supreme Court decision that reaffirmed the result of the 1967 *National Bellas Hess* decision which limits a state's power to require out-of-state mail order companies to collect use tax on their sales to the state's residents. The *Quill* decision did make clear, however, that Congress can enact legislation overturning *National Bellas Hess*. *See also National Bellas Hess* decision, nexus, use tax.

Regressive (tax). A tax that imposes a proportionately heavier burden on low income people than on high income people as a share of their incomes. Sales taxes on groceries are regressive because people spend roughly similar amounts on groceries regardless of income; this means that a larger share of poor people's income goes for groceries.

Separate entity apportionment. *See* combination/combined reporting.

Targeting. The extent to which a program (a tax or an exemption from taxes, for example) reaches its intended beneficiaries as opposed to other people.

Tax expenditure. A provision of a tax law that reduces government revenue through a special exclusion, deduction, deferral, or preferential tax rate.

Tax planning. In this report, the effort by businesses to discover all legal means by which to minimize their state and local tax payments.

Throwback rule. A provision of UDITPA, incorporated in many states' corporate income tax apportionment statutes, that assigns sales to the numerator of the sales factor of the state *from which* the goods are shipped if the state *to which* the goods are delivered does not have jurisdiction to tax that corporation. (If a corporation is taxable in the state to which goods are delivered, those sales are assigned to the sales factor numerator of that "destination state.") The throwback rule is aimed at preventing the creation of "nowhere income" by the non-taxability of a corporation in a state in which it makes sales. Business representatives frequently argue that the throwback rule (and the throwout rule, *see* definition below) are unfair and represent overreaching by the states because the profit is earned in the state in which the customer is located and should not be assigned to another state simply because the corporation is constitutionally or statutorily protected from taxation in that state. *See also:* "nowhere income," origin basis vs. destination basis of sales factor attribution, Public Law 86-272, throwout rule.

Throwout rule. An alternative to the throwback rule. A throwout rule eliminates from both the numerator and denominator of the sales factor any sales made in a state in which a corporation is not taxable. In effect, a throwout rule assigns the profits earned on those sales to the states in which the corporation is taxable in proportion to the *remaining* apportionment factors. The throwback rule, in contrast, assigns those profits all to one state, namely, the state from which the goods are shipped. Advocates of the throwout rule argue that it is more fair to spread the profits among the remaining states than to assign them to the state from which the goods happen to be shipped.

Transfer payments (transfer income). Income received through social insurance and public assistance programs such as Social Security payments, Supplemental Security Income (SSI), food stamps, Medicare and Medicaid coverage, and unemployment insurance.

Transfer price. The price charged for the sale of a product, service, etc. between commonly owned and controlled but legally distinct corporations (e.g., the price that a U.S. parent company manufacturer of computers charges its European wholesale distribution subsidiary). The transfer prices charged can be set to achieve tax minimization goals, among others. If the tax rate in the United States is higher on average than the tax rate in the country in which the European distribution subsidiary's warehouse is located, the manufacturer can set a low sales price so that most of the profit on the sales shows up on the books of the subsidiary. If the U.S. tax rate is lower, the manufacturer can charge a high price to the subsidiary, so only a small profit will appear on the subsidiary's books. Transfer prices can be set in the same manner to take advantage of tax rate differentials between states within the United States.

Section 482 of the Internal Revenue Code authorizes the I.R.S. to establish transfer prices other than those originally set by the corporation and to recompute U.S. tax liability on the basis of the new transfer prices. The I.R.S. regulations implementing Section 482 consider transfer prices to be subject to restatement if they are other than those that would have been charged on the same transaction between unrelated corporations. This "arm's-length standard" for evaluating transfer prices, which is also embodied in U.S. tax treaties with other nations, has long been criticized by certain observers as both unworkable in practice and theoretically flawed. Concern is growing that current efforts to enforce Section 482 are failing to prevent an excessive erosion of the federal corporate income tax base.

UDITPA. The Uniform Division of Income for Tax Purposes Act. A model statute upon which most states' laws for apportioning corporate income are based. UDITPA was developed by the National Conference of

Commissioners on Uniform States Laws in the late 1950s and approved in 1957. A slightly amended version of UDITPA constitutes Article IV of the Multistate Tax Compact, and all Multistate Tax Commission member states permit corporations to apportion income on this basis.

Under UDITPA's formula apportionment approach, a state with jurisdiction to tax a particular corporation applies its tax rate(s) to a percentage of the corporation's total profit, which is calculated by averaging the in-state share of the corporation's total property, payroll and sales. Property, payroll, and sales (or "receipts") are referred to as the three "apportionment factors," and are intended to represent an objective measure of a corporation's in-state activities. The denominator of each factor is the total of that corporation's property value in existence, payroll, payments made, and sales income received everywhere during the tax year. The numerator for each specific state is determined with reference to detailed "attribution rules" that spell out when a particular item of property, wage payment, or sale is deemed to be "in" that particular state.

For example, if 40 percent of Corporation X's total property, 30 percent of its total annual payroll and 20 percent of its total annual sales are "in" State A, State A would tax 30 percent of the corporation's total profit, a figure arrived at by averaging 40 percent, 30 percent and 20 percent. (This example presumes for the sake of simplicity that Corporation X is engaged in a single line of business, i.e., that all of its activities constitute one "unitary business.")

Nearly all states use the sales, payroll, and property factors to apportion corporate income taxes, but an increasing number are giving double or greater weight to the sales factor.

Unitary business. That set of a business' activities that constitute an integrated economic enterprise, regardless of whether the activities are conducted by a single legal entity or multiple legal entities. The clearest example of a set of activities that would generally be conceded to constitute a "unitary business" would be those encompassing a "vertical" production and distribution process within a group of commonly owned and controlled corporations (e.g., oil exploration, production, refining, and distribution of refined products). Another clear example would be a business operating supermarkets in multiple locations but purchasing inventory for most of the stores at the same time and from the same suppliers.

The U.S. Supreme Court has made clear that to determine corporate income tax liability through apportionment, a state may only apportion the income of a unitary business that is being conducted in part in the state. For example, suppose a corporation has two different lines of business— steelmaking and running a department store. If there are no significant economic ties between them and if only the department store does business in state A, then state A may apportion only the profits of the department store. Conversely, a state may add the profit of an out-of-state corporation over which it has no taxing jurisdiction to the profit of a corporation over which it has such jurisdiction for purposes of determining the latter's in-state taxable income through apportionment if (and only if) the out-of-state corporation is engaged in a unitary business with the in-state corporation. (This explains why this practice æ"combined reporting"æis often referred to as "unitary combination"; the authority for the combination for state tax purposes of the profits of legally-distinct entities rests on the entities being engaged in a unitary business.)

Determination of whether a single corporation or a group of corporations is engaged in a single or multiple "unitary businesses" is a fact-intensive exercise that sometimes leads to disputes between taxpayers and state tax authorities. When confronted with a dispute, the courts have applied a variety of legal tests to establish the boundaries of a unitary business. While sometimes difficult to apply in practice, the general concept is reasonably clear, namely, that the centralized coordination of a set of activities arguably enables the enterprise to earn greater profits than would be earned by completely separate companies engaged in the same activities. Common sources of this "synergistic" effect on profitability include technical economies of scale, ability to take advantage of quantity discounts on inputs, ability to maintain higher utilization of expensive fixed production capacity, ability to overcome capital market imperfections, information economies, etc. *See also* combined reporting/ combination.

Use tax. Also frequently referred to as a "compensating use tax." A tax generally levied at the same rate and on the same base as the sales tax on the use, consumption, or storage of goods and services in a state (and, where applicable, locality). A compensating use tax is required to be paid by customers who purchase goods outside the state and then bring them into the state for use, storage, etc. States are also beginning to levy use taxes on services that are obtained from out-of-state providers but consumed in-state.

The use tax is levied to eliminate the incentive to buy goods (and services) in states where they are taxed at a lower rate or not taxed at all. If the goods and services have not been taxed at all, the full amount of the tax is due. It the goods and services have been taxed at a lower rate, use tax is effectively due only at a rate equal to the difference in rates. If sales tax has been paid at the place of purchase equal or greater than the use tax, most states will not charge additional use tax. *See also* nexus, *National Bellas Hess* decision, *Quill* decision.

User charges or fees. Direct charges for the use of public goods or services, such as admission to park, tuition at a state university, or charges at a public hospital.

Vertical equity. Refers to the way that households or taxpayers of different incomes or levels of resources are treated by a program or tax. Evaluations of a tax as either progressive, proportional, or regressive are measurements of its vertical equity.